Memories of a Gypsy

Memories of a Gypsy

Victor Vishnevsky

SALO
PRESS

2006

Salo Press
5607 Greenleaf Road
Cheverly, Maryland 20785

Printed in the United States of America

Library of Congress Control Number: 2006930877

ISBN 0-9787728-0-6
ISBN-13 978-0-9787728-0-2

The original manuscript of this book was written in English and com-pleted September 29, 1999. A translation into Portuguese was pub-lished in São Paulo, Brazil, in 1999 by Duna Dueto Editora Ltda. (ISBN 85-87308-01-4). The present edition was prepared directly from the original English-language manuscript.

Cover and photo editing, Martha Newberry.

I dedicate this book to my beloved wife, my sons and daughters, and especially to my grandchildren, so that they may give this book to their children, and their children's children. I know that they will have a better tomorrow, and may God bless them all.

My story began in 1938 in Shanghai, China, as far as my memory can reach. I remember that I was in the middle of a conflict between Japan and China. Of course I actually I did not understand what was going on. What seems to be alive in my mind, the "dogfights" in the air, the bombings, the trucks carrying dead bodies by the hundreds, while the blood was dribbling on the asphalt, right in the middle of the French Concession, Shanghai city.

I must explain that Shanghai was considered an international city due to the so-called Boxer Rebellion. The Boxers war, as it was called, started sometime in the beginning of the twentieth century. Actually it was not a war, but an uprising by the local sect called the Boxers. The empress dowager Tz'u-hsi was said to be the head of the movement. The main cause of the movement was to rid China of foreigners, especially the missionaries who were spread all over China, spreading Christianity. That made the queen, who was Buddhist, very upset about the situation. At that time she was at the capital of China, by the name of Beijing, which up to this day it keeps this name. In Beijing all the foreign embassies were assembled, and were situated at a small villa called by the name of legation. Slowly but surely the killings of the missionaries started, and it began to spread like fire. When the embassies complained about the situation, the queen said that she did not know anything about it. But the Boxers were known by their uniforms. They were wearing red bands around their heads, and were mostly dressed in red. The situation was terrible. When they surrounded the embassies, and did not let them out of the villa, immediately the embassies organized to protect themselves from the imminent danger. They did what they could, but they knew that in time, they may all be killed, so somehow they asked help from their respective governments headed by the English. Just in time the forces of England, Russia, America, and Japan, and many other countries, came and defeated the Boxers in the capital of Beijing, and the interior of the countries. For punishment the government of China had to give some semi-colonies to the countries mentioned above. That is why Shanghai, China, and a few other cities were given to these countries to rule. This version of the story was told to me by my elders.

The City of Shanghai, China, was divided between the English and the French. My family was located in the French Concession. There was no frontier between them. All you had to do is cross the street, and you were in the English Concession. You recognized the difference only by the uniforms of the police. If you committed a crime of some sort on the French side and crossed the street to the English side no one could touch you unless the French police asked a special permission to get you. The French law prevailed in their concession and the English in theirs, and they lived side by side in peace and prosperity.

My youth was always involved with wars. I can say that I almost got used to it, but nevertheless I had a certain fear I could not understand. By the time the Second World War arrived, I could call myself a war veteran.

I was born to a Gypsy family in Shanghai. My parents ran away from Russia due to the civil war. Ever since I can remember we were in show business. I loved to watch my father and my sisters doing the show. Of course there were other Gypsies included in the show, we were considered the best group in China. Before long my father owned his nightclub, which was called "The Black Eyes;" it was even known in New York.

My father always wanted me to go to school, unlike the other Gypsy boys. I was the only boy in the family, and the youngest. We had a few adventures worth to be registered.

One beautiful night, I and some other Gypsy boys were playing on the streets near my house when all of a sudden there were explosions in the air. The sound was the familiar anti-aircraft cannons, but this time something different happened. An explosion of bigger dimension exploded right above our heads, the impact threw all of us to the ground with considerable force. Within seconds I heard a terrible scream a few feet away from me. I got up to my feet a little dazed from the impact. When I reached to my friend, there were some other boys already there, gazing down at him. One of his leg was covered with blood. Then I noticed that the other leg was only connected to his ankle by his skin. The shock I got was terrible. I was shaking all over, then there was a lot of confusion around us. I know I was one of the boys who carried the wounded boy to my house, because it was the nearest. From there on some of our elders took him to the hospital, naturally his leg was amputated. That night there were other victims, but all of them were Chinese. The one and only Gypsy victim throughout the Second World War.

I must say we were lucky, as far as casualties are concerned. In Shanghai there were a lot of bombings, usually by the so-called Flying Fortresses, also known as B-29, but thank God they never bombed the International Concession. That doesn't mean that they did not make mistakes, every now and than they would release their bombs in the wrong places. That is why I hardly believe that there may be a durable peace in this world. Mistakes are always done, and innocent people pay for it.

During the Japanese occupation life wasn't so bad compared to Europe, lets say it was livable. Yes, we were short of food and all other things that are needed in life. Of course I am referring to my family, thanks to the Swiss Red Cross which helped us once a month. Because we were Iranian subjects, we were given by the Japanese government red bands to wear on our arms. That identified us as second-class enemies. We had no right to leave town or go to any public places. We were also issued bread coupons, but it was in small amounts. Little by little we sold everything we had of value, and by the time the war was nearing to its end we had almost nothing left. The funny thing about China was that even a pair of old socks could be sold, anything had its price. I never passed hunger because my mother always had something for me to eat. Just to give the reader an idea, my father was a big man, he was about 120 kilos, he came down to 80 kilos, for short the whole Gypsy clan looked underfed.

I will never forget when we went to a Russian club to play bingo, the announcer stopped in the middle of the game, and then a man came and whispered in his ear. Suddenly he shouted with all his strength, "It is capitulation, capitulation." I did not know what it meant, but all the people around me stood up and began to cheer, hugging and kissing each other, including my parents, when I asked what was going on, they said the war is over.

I would very much like to go back in the past for a few years, so that the reader would know what was happening during the occupation of the Japanese forces. Naturally in the following lines I was told by my parents because I was too young to understand. To begin with I was told the Japanese were not so evil as we expected, on the contrary they never bothered us Gypsies or the White Russians because we were all refugees from communist Russia, unless you had something to do with politics, or dealt with black market material, like all type of metals or gasoline which was absolutely taboo.

For local transportation we used a tricycle we called pedicabs, sort of a taxi, enough to carry two passengers. There were cars, but very rare, and they did not run by gasoline but by wood. The cars had a big stove mounted on the back of the car, then wood was stuffed into the stove and lit up, that was the energy needed to make the car run. Logically there were a lot of fires with this cars, I myself saw some of them.

The black market was flourishing, with money you could buy anything, except items I mentioned above, but if you were caught, nobody knew what would happen to you. There was a big building over the Whangpoo river, that divided Shanghai of the French and English concessions, which was called the Bridge House. This building was feared throughout Shanghai. I was told that anyone who got arrested, and got into it, would never see the sun again. Or who did come out, would live a few days and die. The only person I know that survived was one of our Gypsies. He was a good dancer. He also was a good friend of a very famous Russian singer by the name of Vertinsky who some how managed to escape to Russia via Vladivostok. He was accused of spying for the Russians. Naturally as this Gypsy being his friend, he was arrested. He was also accused of spying. Only God knows what made them release him, maybe because he was a Gypsy, and the whole world knows that Gypsies do not get involved in politics. Later we were told that Vertinsky bought a war tank for the Russian front, and Stalin, the Russian leader, thanked him for that. After the war this was confirmed by some Russians who received letters from Russia. Vertinsky was actually a spy almost all through the war. He worked and lived among us, and nobody knew or suspected that he had anything to do with politics. Anyway, the poor Gypsy dancer lived a few weeks and died.

But let's talk about myself. I went to a French school which was called St. Jeanne d'Arc; it was a Catholic school run by fathers and brothers. I studied there up to the fourth grade. I could have studied more, but unfortunately my father could not afford it any longer. So I was transferred to a Russian Catholic school, where the father was a friend of ours, and he agreed to teach me for free. His name was Father Wilcock, he was a very good man, and he was building a new school. The school was ready in about a couple of weeks. One day he came and told us that the Japanese had announced in the local newspaper that all new buildings should be handed over to them. They did not give the reason why, so if and when the day arrived, Father Wilcock was desperate. He decided to take all his pupils to sleep in the school, so that the Japanese would think that it was an orphanage and have pity on us. I don't know where he arranged so many beds, we were about twenty-five students. We were told we should stay there until the Japanese would come to inspect the school. Of course with the permission of our parents. I remember we had a good time in the room that we were installed. It was large, all twenty-five of us were accommodated there. All of us spoke in Russian or English, so it was easy to communicate among ourselves.

There was a big stove right in the middle of the room. During the night we used to play Red Indians, circling the red hot stove, and imitating Red Indian dancing. Then one night as we were playing, one of the boys hit the other with the pillow. That all was needed to start a fight among us. I will never forget the scene, the pillows started to burst from all parts of the room, and it looked like it was snowing in the room. As I was one of the youngest, I hid myself under the bed, Within a few minutes the door of the room burst open, and Father Wilcock stood there, he had a bamboo stick in his hand. All I heard was, "Stop, you little hooligans," and he waved the bamboo stick in the air. Everybody stopped as if by magic. "So this is the way you all have come to help me to save this school from the Japanese." Nobody said a word, then he opened the lights, and then told for all to stand in line, and spoke again. "Do you know what is at stake, your very future is at stake, education after God is every thing in life." I remember that I was stunned by his voice. I was expecting something more drastic, but to my surprise he took a deep breath, and kept quiet for a moment and said, "All of you start cleaning the mess up, and I don't care how much time it takes," then turned on his heels, opened the door and walked away. We all started to work almost 'til the morning, and then went to bed, of course without the pillows under our heads.

Within a few hours the bell rang, we had be on our feet and ready for inspection, we all looked tired and half asleep. Just as we were getting in line, a group of Japanese officers entered the hall without being announced. It took us all by surprise; the fathers—there were others besides Wilcock—were visibly upset, especially Father Wilcock. He looked very pale, and looked sick, to me he instantly lost his leadership to the Japanese officers. I always had an utmost respect and admiration for that priest. But now he looked like any other helpless human being. The fathers greeted the Japanese with utmost respect, and bowing their heads, that looked lower than necessary, and repeating the bows several times, to make it seem more respectable. I don't even know how the other students felt, but I was scared like hell. They spoke for a few minutes, then the officers came over to inspect us, they spoke a little among themselves, to us it seemed like an eternity, then they came over to us again, gave us a big salute, went to the fathers, and said something to them, and walked away. A few minutes passed before we could come to our senses, then I heard the word, "Miracle, a miracle has happened, the school is saved." After this tremendous event, we were all allowed to go home.

But before we left, we were told that tomorrow we will all have a party, including our parents, to celebrate the event. When we arrived on the feast, I was astonished of the amount of food and drinks available. I don't know were the fathers managed to arrange all of the stuff. Anyway, we all ate as we never did before. Father Wilcock made a speech thanking our parents and us, for collaborating with them, and promising us that the school, will start next Monday.

I was very excited about my going to school when it officially opened, but I did not know that something bad would happen to me. When I arrived in school, there were new teachers appointed, they were civilian teachers. I found myself in a class much higher than I was supposed to be. The subject was mathematics, what he wrote on the black board, looked like Greek to me, when my turn came to go to the blackboard, I told him that I did not know what was written on the board. I don't know what happened to him, all of sudden he got red in the face, started to shout at me. I did not know what he said, but I knew what was coming. He had a big bamboo rod in his hand, and before long I was bent on his knee, and he brought down the rod on my behind, God knows how many times. I ran out of the class, it was very painful, I could hardly run, but I made it to my home. When my mother saw me she asked me what happened. I could not talk, I showed her my behind. When she took off my pants, and saw the damage done by the rod, she screamed, and started to cry. She immediately took me to a nearby pharmacy to treat my wounds. "The teacher must be a maniac," she said, and then my mother took me back to the school, and we went straight to Father Wilcock's office. When my mother showed my wounds to the priest, he was astonished. He called the teacher and said that he would put him in jail, and it was just what he did. My wounds were so severe that I had to be hospitalized for several days. I studied there up 'til the end of the war.

I had quite a happy youth, not only Gypsy friends, but also foreign friends, my best foreign friend was Rony Macintosh, he was living just across the road from where I lived, in a big apartment building called the Saint Paul's. Of course he was English. There was a big playground in front of his apartment, we spent hours playing football and other games. There was also a few English young girls who played with us. I shall never forget Norma, she was a few years older than me, she was special to me, I think she was my first childish love. I did every thing in my power to please her. I think she sensed it, because I was always there to serve her. When the Japanese came to take the English and other war enemies to concentration camps, they gave only a few hours notice, it was a very sad day for me. I remember I wanted to give her a present so that she would think of me, but unfortunately I had nothing to give. I went up to her and said, "Norma I have nothing to give you for remembrance." She smiled and said, "I understand," and then to my surprise she kissed me. "I shall never forget you, Gypsy boy," and started to cry. All of a sudden I had an idea. I had a white hanky in my pocket. I took it out right in front of her, then I put my wrist to the wall, which was a very rough cement, then I brushed against it with all my strength. Immediately my wrist was bleeding. I wrapped the hanky around my wrist and held it for a while, 'til the hanky was quite stained with my blood. She cried out, "No, no," but it was too late, it was already done. Then she said, "Why did you do that?" I said, "Norma, this is all I have to give you." I extended the hanky to her, at first she hesitated, but then she took it, and said that she would keep it forever, than she abruptly turned away and ran away, but before she went away there were still tears in her eyes. That was the last time I ever saw her again, or Rony Macintosh. They were taken away that very afternoon, they must be somewhere in England.

Now I will take the reader just a week or so before the Second World War was over. We all suspected that something was wrong. One morning we awakened to see Japanese soldiers un-armed, sitting on the sidewalk with earphones attached to their heads, and listening to their radios. We did not know it then, but it must have been the Emperor Hirohito announcing the ca-pitulation after the atomic bombs had been dropped. A few days later we were told at the bingo game of the capitulation.

I remember that the first contact with the US forces was when two DC-3 planes appeared out of nowhere in the sky over the French Concession, at first we thought it was Japanese air craft, and besides, there was no siren. They were quite high, but slowly by slowly they came lower and lower, as if waiting for the Japanese to open fire, it was a test. When there was no response, they started to throw small parachutes, hundreds of them. We kids ran out to catch some of the parachutes that came our way, I myself caught a few of them. The Chinese did not dare come near them. Oh, yes, we had quite a ball that day.

The parachutes were not the conventional type, they were very small, enough to carry about 4 kilos. The contents of the package, logically, was food, among other things, to be exact it was army rations, from chocolate to cigarettes, canned beef, and other canned goods, including pudding. The first liberation army to arrive was Chinese Chiang Kai-shek special forces.

Almost overnight, the climate of Shanghai changed. There was everything you wanted to buy in the city, from where it all appeared only God knows. Within weeks, the Seventh US Fleet was anchored in the Whangpoo River which divided the city.

In no time nearly every shop turned into a bar, including my father, he also opened a bar. It was such a success, within a few months we had another bar open. It was said that almost seven thousand sailors a night visited the bars and nightclubs, not to mention the soldiers, and the air force personnel stationed ashore. The city was lighted up with various colored neon lights, particularly our French area, to me it was Paradise. After so many years of blackouts, during the war, it was wonderful to be alive.

I was almost fourteen years old, and was already helping my father with our Gypsy music band. I already knew how to play accordion. As the saying goes, that we Gypsies have music in our blood. I quickly learned the new songs that the Americans brought with them. I can say that I was popular amongst the Americans who visited our bar, and they were many, both our bars were full. Every night including Sundays. Of course we had young girls behind the bar, most of them Russian. There was nobody to check whether they were underage, so mostly the girls were in their teens. Generally their families did not object, because of the dollars they brought home. I really could not blame them, after what they went through the war.

In no time everyone had money, work, and on top of that the Americans issued army rations to all foreigners living in Shanghai. The life became easy, nobody talked about food anymore, everybody wanted to make dollars, even the rickshaws and pedicabs were full of dollars. The American sailors spent their money as if it was paper. After so many years not getting paid, this was no surprise.

But there was also some trouble. The married women who left their husbands, and went to work in bars or nightclubs, were often beaten, and very severely, by their husbands, sometimes even murder committed. But to no avail, the women in Shanghai went crazy, with young good looking sailors available, and ready to spend money by the tons. What woman could resist? Within a year things began to change. I personally think the sailors went out of control, and almost became hooligans. There was constantly fights in the bars amongst themselves, or sailors vs. soldiers, or civilians. The MP and the SP were not enough to stop them because they were so many. Before long, half of the bars were out of bounds, including our two bars. One was destroyed, the other was out of bounds for good.

Then we heard something about the Cold War, and also about the communist forces in the far north of China. This changed things for the Gypsy and Russian communities.

The Cold War was between the Americans and the Russians, and who controlled Shanghai was the Americans, but not officially. We Gypsies did not feel its effect 'til it got difficult to find jobs because the Americans were ordered not to mix any more with the local Russians or Gypsies or any other foreigners in Shanghai. That made life more difficult. But by this time many Russians in Shanghai got rich and owned their own nightclubs, and also the local Chinese made business with us, so it was not too bad, we did not need anymore the Americans for survival. But the threat of the communists was imminent.

The main reason of the cold war, was that the communists wanted a world-wide communism and at that time the Russians did not have the atomic bomb. The Russians were afraid that the Americans might use the atomic bomb on them.

The local Russians in Shanghai, China, most of them, were without any documents. Some of them applied for passports in the Soviet embassy. As far as my family was concerned, we all were Iranian subjects. There was no Iranian consulate in Shanghai, the Indian embassy was in charge of our affairs.

We lived for almost thirty years with our local Gypsies, they were all from a different tribe called the Kelderasa. They were, or are, more conservative than us Lovara, their women still wore the traditional Gypsy robes, and they never let their children go to schools, particularly females. The reason was not to have marriages with other races, to keep the race intact. Oh yes, we have our differences, the only thing we have in common is the language, and of course the music, there is a bit of difference in the language, but its usually understandable. All Gypsies mix up some words with the language of the country were they were born, or lived for some decades.

11

Generally people look upon us as a mysterious race, as a matter of fact we are a mysterious race. Nobody knows our origin, but I have reason to believe that we are from India. Later on I shall relate to my reader the reason of believing in this theory. We Gypsies are not what most people think we are. Throughout the centuries the people of all nations looked upon us like we were misplaced persons who had no country and had no one to protect us, so anything bad that happened was blamed on the Gypsies, like robbing children and cheating. But what a Gypsy needs to steal a child for when we have more than enough of our own? We Gypsies are almost like the northwestern Brazilians who have at least five to six children in a normal family.

As for cheating, it's usually related to fortune telling. When she or he comes to a Gypsy fortune teller, naturally she or he has a problem, usually it's a health problem, domestic problems, not to mention a hundred more problems that life usually brings to us. Now why do they come to us? As I have already mentioned, we are a mysterious people, throughout the centuries people know that we are good at telling fortunes. Now if the fortune teller tells the truth or not, it's only for the person that is seeking for help to decide! Have my readers ever went to a church, and said their confession to the priest? Well, that's the way that our fortune telling works, some people get a relief when they confess to the priest. This is just one of the examples. There are head doctors, we call them shrinks, that put you on a couch and ask you a million questions, and then after a while he says that you are cured, well this is more or less the way our fortune tellers are! Some are good at it and some are not. Mostly all of them try their best way to get the client back on the track of his life, they argue that life is not easy, but if she or he will listen to her advice they might overcome their troubles. As for the future, a good fortune teller might see it by the story that the client has told her, like a good philosopher of the Middle Ages. Today thousands of non-Gypsies took up our profession through the television, propaganda, etc., etc., and it is all legal, and every one claims to be better than the other! As the Bible says, beware of false prophets.

We are not different from any other minority people in this world. Yes, we have our bad elements like any other minority, which is usually blamed for anything bad that goes on in the country, for example the Afro-Americans and the Afro-Brazilians, and also the so called Chicanos, American-Mexican mixture that the statistics say that they have the highest number of crime, in the whole world, including assassinations, not to mention drug trafficking, rape, etc., etc. This is called pure discrimination as far as Gypsies are concerned.

As the cold war got colder, the Soviet leader Stalin decided to pardon all the refugees from Russia, and told them to come home who wanted to. So most of our Gypsy friends decided to accept his generosity. Stalin even sent ships to evacuate the refugees, I even remember one of the ships' names, it was the Smolny. When the time to part came, there was always farewell parties. Some families were divided, because somehow they did not get in the same group which was about to leave, so there was a lot of confusion. Some thought that the ship will not come back, and some even thought that they will be shot there, for some reason or another. There were about ten to fifteen families who were about to leave, mostly Kelderasa tribe. We went to see them off on the wharf. There was always spectacular behavior by those families left behind, they brought a lot of vodka and food with them, they ate and drank and we also accompanied them, and as almost all of us are musicians, we brought our musical instruments with us, and made music right on the wharf. So you can imagine what fun we had, there was singing dancing and crying. The other passengers, all White Russians, also joined us, almost everybody knew everybody else, we lived a lot of years together, only God knows what we all went through. So we all suffered to see our friends, and even in some cases sweethearts, leaving us for good.

There is a funny story that I shall relate to the reader, that some families, before leaving, decided to unite, and created some sort of secret code, such as on arrival to the USSR, they would send back letters, but knowing that the letters will be censored, they included photographs in the letters. The code was as follows. If he or she were standing in the photograph, that means life was all right. If they were in a sitting position, life was bad. When the letters arrived, they were surprised to see that their families in the photographs were all in a lying position. You can just imagine what a shock they got. But nevertheless their loved ones were there, so they had to join them, for the better or the worse. But as far as I know, it was terrible. Of course we found out much later, after one or two Russians managed to escape and related many horrible stories about how they were treated in the USSR.

They were considered a little less than enemies. The fact that they were renegades from their homeland did not affect the Soviet Russians so much, but what made them hate the renegades, was that they did not participate in the war, and did not suffer so much as they did, but came to enjoy the victory, which was not theirs to enjoy. Many old White Russian ex-officers of the Imperial Army were shot, these poor souls thought that time was their salvation, but unfortunately, they underestimated the communist regime. Even before they arrived their records were selected and waited for them, everybody's life story was carefully scrutinized. They were mostly all divided and sent to Siberian coal mines, except for the few who were highly educated, and were needed in Moscow to be used for the communist cause.

The communist is a totalitarian country. I will try to explain to the reader how this system worked. The father of communism is said to be Karl Marx, but who installed the communist regime in Russia was Lenin and Stalin, Trotsky, etc., etc. Their proposition to the masses of the Russian people, and the world, was to liquidate capitalism. Lenin saw to it that the royal family of Russia was liquidated, he abolished all types of religion, confiscated all private property, and prohibited freedom of speech and the freedom of the press and movement, not to mention the millions of prisoners he has sent to the Siberian camps for hard labor. Just to give an idea to the reader, the temperature in Siberia goes down to almost forty degrees below zero! Imagine, who would not be afraid from such a regime? And the Gypsies love freedom above all things, this type of government meant hell to us. The downfall of the communism in Russia started with the death of its leader Stalin, but not until Kruschchev was the head of the regime, and accused Stalin of his crimes and the mass destruction of his people during his reign, to his people, but what helped bring down the Russian communists, was without doubt the great *perestroika*, headed by the leader Gorbachev (*perestroika* means reform} and of course the falling of the Berlin wall that divided Germany.

But the most dangerous thing during the cold war was when Krushchev brought his nuclear missiles to communist Cuba, who is headed by the communist leader Fidel Castro, who 'til this day is still the leader in Cuba. Krushchev did this to threaten the USA. As you may know, Cuba is only a hundred and sixty odd kilometers from the USA. That was during the Kennedy administration in the USA. That's when a nuclear war nearly started, and could have been the end of this world, but good sense prevailed, and thanks God this is history now.

Only a few of our Gypsy friends were sent to Moscow, because they were exceptional musicians. Many years later we heard that many died, very few survived, and left Siberia, and came to other parts of Russia.

My family and other relatives decided to travel to Hong Kong. On the eve of the New Year of 1949, still in Shanghai, we all, I mean my parents, celebrated the New Year's eve in a Russian club. That's were I met my first wife, Tamara, she was working there as a waitress. As Gypsy artists, naturally we were asked to give a show, and so we did, it was a complete success. I was told later by my wife that there she fell in love with me. She practically seduced me that night, not that I was timid, Gypsy youngsters are rarely are, and I am no exception. One thing led to another, before I knew it I was hooked.

Another thing I must explain to the reader. We Gypsies get married very early, especially the males. This is why I think we have a very few homosexuals among our race. Our elders practically force us to go out and have sex after our fifteenth birthday, so that we have more experience in sex when we get married, and also avoid to have gay tendencies. I cannot be sure if the scheme works, but one thing is sure, I met a lot of Gypsies around the world of all tribes, and I heard of only few cases.

My wife Tamara was a half-caste, her father was Chinese and her mother, Russian. I was only seventeen and she was eighteen when we married. The marriage was Gypsy-style, we invited some important Gypsy people, threw a party, made it official, and that was all there was. No church ceremony, no official documents of the event, we were just man and wife in the eyes of our people. That's how my father wanted it, but at my age it was fun for just a while. Soon I wanted my freedom. I had a Gypsy girl on my mind. Yes, she was beautiful, her name was Aza. She was from a different tribe, the tribe we Lovara usually got married to by tradition, of course, if our women were not available.

The real way of a Gypsy marriage is completely different, and it is valid up 'til today. The father of the young man usually chooses the young girl for his son. The first thing what he does when he finds the ideal girl for his son, is to go to the girl's father with a bottle of wine with a golden coin attached to it with a red ribbon. Of course, he does not go alone, he invites his best friends to accompany him to the girl's house. One of his friends must be a good orator to convince the father of the girl to give away his daughter. But mostly all of this time the father of the girl knew that one day this man will come to ask his daughter's hand, because of the gossip, but he pretends that it came as a surprise. The bottle of wine with the gold coin is the symbol that the man has come to ask his daughter's hand. It is a small party. When the orator sees that it is time to come to the subject, he always begins by saying that the family of the boy is from a noble descent, and is doing well in life, including that his son is a good worker in what ever he does, then the orator usually asks permission if the father is willing to give away his daughter. When they come to an understanding they set a date for the official engagement. It was usually done in their houses, but today they hire a club and if the man is rich, two to three hundred people are invited. The father of the son pays all the expenses.

At the engagement they start to argue about the price of the bride, but this all is symbolic, the price is already known, it is five Austrian gold coins, but the father asks, let's say, for twenty gold coins, but then he begins to come down with the price, as it's the custom. For the honor of his brother he takes down five coins, then he does the same for his best friends, until he comes to the amount of the five coins, that everybody knows that this is the actual price. When all this is finished he puts a necklace of gold coins on the bride's neck. Then every thing is official, she already belongs to the young man, but she will be his only after the wedding. The date is set according to the wish of the girl's father, but it is never more then a month or so. Besides the food of the club, which is a normal food that any restaurant offers, they bring with them the traditional Gypsy food. The most favorite is called *salmaia*, it is made of stuffed cabbage with meat and rice, in it. Then comes the fried pigs in a big quantity, and also fried sheep. The table must be full to capacity, otherwise it will be an insult to the girl's father. For drinks you will find almost all types, but beer is the favorite, at least in São Paulo, but in other countries they drink the best local drinks what the country can offer.

On the wedding day the bride must wear white as in any Catholic manner, but the main thing that bride must have is white underwear, because when she will go to bed with her husband she must show that she is a virgin, and the stain of the blood must be visible on her underwear. On the wedding there must be red flags indicating symbolically the virginity of the bride, the bridesmaids usually carry them. The father hires musicians for the event, and of course we have our own musicians, so we have two different types of music, of the country that we are in, and our traditional Gypsy music. When the bride and the groom go home for the first night, they are accompanied by the oldest ladies, so that they may be the witnesses of her virginity by sitting just outside the bed room until the job is done. Then the bride gives her underwear to the old ladies to show it on the other day of the wedding. Yes, it takes two days for the wedding to be complete, the last day is the most important because they bring the cloth stained with the blood of the virgin for every one to see. Before, they used to collect money or gold articles from the guests as presents for bride and groom, but today they don't do it anymore. The reason is simple, when one puts more money in the basket which usually the bride goes around to collect with it, the other guests who cannot afford to put that much as the other, he gets offended, and that's were the quarrel starts, and there might be fights, so this is avoided.

Going back to my marriage, she somehow conquered my father's heart, she was always there to serve him tea, to read the Chinese newspaper to him, which was very important, because the Red Army was coming closer to Shanghai.

There were very little Russians left in Shanghai after 1949, because many of them applied to the American- backed IRO organization and were sent to an island called Samar, in the Philippines. We also heard a lot of rumors that many people died there of malaria and the heat while awaiting their transportation to the States.

As I already mentioned, our plan was to cross the border to Hong Kong, China. The Red Army just occupied Nanking, that's about two to three hundred kilometers from Shanghai, so we decided to leave as soon as possible. We were about seven to eight families, totaling to more or less thirty-five to forty persons, between children, women, and men. The trains were still running between Shanghai and Canton, China. The city of Canton is just about seventy kilometers from Hong Kong, it is situated south of Shanghai. The trains were precarious. From Shanghai to Canton it takes about forty-eight hours to travel the distance between the two cities, but it took us five long days to make it there. Logically, all well-to-do Chinese people, and mostly the middle class, were running away from the advancing Red Army. The trains were full to capacity. I remember I had to bribe the station master to obtain the tickets. In every big station we waited, nobody knows for whom or for what, we waited so long, every time the train started to move again there was a great relief, because everybody thought that the Red Army would invade the train any minute. Nobody really knew were the Red Army was, near or far, the tension was extremely hard to control. Oh yes, we took some food with us, but we did not expect the train to take so long to take us to our destination, so we were obliged to buy food from the local stations. We could not dare to leave the train even for a minute, for we never knew when the train might leave. The food we bought was good for the elders, but for the children, we had a hard time to convince them to eat.

Anyway we arrived safely. The very next day we took another train for the border between China and the British colony of Hong Kong. We were all excited because freedom was so close, yet I remember something bothered me. We passed the Chinese border without any trouble, but when we reached the British border we were asked to show our documents. A young officer looked through our documents and then looked again, as if something was missing in our passports, and indeed it was. He said the visa was missing to enter the colony, we all protested but all in vain. He insisted that as we are Iranian subjects and we have to have visas to enter the colony. He advised us to return to Canton and go to the British consulate and apply for a visa. We told him that the Red Army was getting closer to Canton and that it was dangerous, because there was panic and disorder going on in Canton, but to no avail. We had to return under any circumstances. When we returned to Canton, to our misery the British consulate refused us our visas because our passports were outdated. We had no choice but to find a new way out.

After studying a lot of Chinese maps we found the nearest border was Burma. We were told that we could cross the border as refugees of the civil war, it was not easy but it was the only way out. We still had money but for how long will it last? We had a lot of luggage. Thanks to the local coolies who work at the train stations or bus stations, they helped us carry our things, which were very heavy. We practically did not leave nothing behind, the only valuable thing we left behind was our residence. And so this is how our adventure started.

We had to take a train a couple of hundred kilometers back to where we came from. I don't remember the city's name, but that's the place where another railroad line took us to Kweilin and the road to Burma.

When we reached the other railway station we had a shock. The trains were completely stuffed by the fleeing National Army, civilians were not allowed to come near the trains, which were surrounded by soldiers, nobody dared to ask for tickets. We went to the station master and told him our situation, he told us our only hope was the general. As my wife was our interpreter and spoke fluently Chinese, naturally she was elected to go and try to convince the general to let us proceed on our journey as refugees going back to our country. So she went to the blockade and asked to see the general. The soldier was surprised to see a young, good-looking woman seeking to speak to the general, he must have thought that she was his girl friend or something, he immediately called an officer who also talked to her a few minutes, and then walked away towards what seemed to be the general's office. I remember the suspense we all went through, we all knew that to be permitted to travel on this army-infested train would be a miracle. I know that mostly all of us silently prayed for the miracle to happen. She was called by the officer to the office, and within ten minutes, what seemed an eternity to us, she came to us with the officer and announced, not only we were allowed to travel but even a special place was arranged for us on the train. From then on she was a sort of a manager representing all of us, the soldiers even helped us carry our baggage to the train, and believe you me we had a lot of it.

On the train we had an incident. About an hour before reaching Kweilin one of the wheels of a wagon, just two wagons in front of us, broke free, we all felt the impact, but luckily the wagon was in the middle of train, the outcome of the incident was minimum. We waited for twenty-four hours before we could start our journey again.

When we reached Kweilin we were almost out of local money. We had dollars, but they were hardly accepted, so we decided to do something about it. We had all our musical instruments and all our show costumes, all we needed was a few rehearsals, and to rent a theater. We decided to go to the local city hall and ask for permission to give a show, despite of the situation. To our surprise not only did he agree, he helped us rent the theater and made a deal with the owner to pay us fifty percent of the box office money. We did not invest a cent. But this was not a nightclub, we had to hold the show for at least an hour and a half, we had to invent some numbers. My sister Lida was good at inventing numbers; she was the star of the show. Of course we had to hire a couple of local artists, like magicians and fire eaters, and also a clown, mostly to tell jokes while the artists changed their costumes. I don't know how, but we managed to hold the spectators for two solid hours. To our surprise it was a complete success, it paid our food, hotel, and even a little bit over for our minor expenses. Naturally I was leading the musical part, without me the show could not go on, I was indispensable. I must admit that I was proud about it. The simple country people were astonished just to see white women and men singing and dancing, it was amazing to see their faces. I was studying their reactions, to them we had come from another world, their eyes shined and their faces radiated with pleasure. Every night was full house. Later on we found out that they opened a hole in the wall, and crawled in to avoid paying the tickets, so simple and yet not innocent, this I could not understand.

The going was good while it lasted, but the commies were always on our heels, we had to move. This time there were no trains. We had to travel by bus. The going was hard for the elders, even the young suffered, only the children seemed to have fun, from all these bumpy roads. The reason we were traveling by bus was not because we liked it, but because most of railroad bridges were exploded by the local communist partisans to avoid the retreat of some National Army forces.

When we arrived in Luchow we already knew how to arrange work. We immediately went to see the mayor of the city, of course Tamara was heading the delegation, me and other elders. He not only agreed, but also invited us for dinner. We dressed as well as possible and went to his palace. When we entered I was stunned of the luxury in the palace, the place was full of Chinese art pieces of all kinds imaginable, there was also a lot of boxes in the corridor sealed off and ready to be taken away any minute, God knows what they contained. We were asked to join him in a big hall also richly decorated with art, we then had a drink before having dinner. The dinner was excellent. I must say I never ate such food in any restaurant or any other place, they served so many dishes that I just could not count them. They came in silver plates even the chop sticks were silver, united by a tiny silver chain. For a Chinese he was quite tall, his wife was

also present. She was a very beautiful women in he
was almost fiftyish and still radiated her beauty, th(
well in English and obviously were from the high
openly talked about the situation in China and said tha
leave in the near future. He also said that helping us was his duty
for humanitarian reasons. To our surprise he handed an envelope
to my wife and said, "This is for your expenses," and as long as
he will be present he would do anything in his power to help us,
"in a way we are both in a same position, we have to leave the
country, but it hurts me more because the country I have to leave
is mine." I could see the emotion in his speech, it moved us all.
He stood up and said, "Let's not think about it, how about having a pipe of opium? It's good for digestion." We gently refused
and asked for a drink instead. We left the palace upset, we hardly
talked to each other on the way to the hotel, I could have sworn
we had all the same thought, how could such a man of his status can be compared to us? But he was right, in war there is no
status, he was to become a refugee as much as we were. With his
help we staged our show, when we finished he even bought us
tickets on the bus, this time for the city of Kunming.

This was a big city, the population was over a million. On
the map we saw that this was the last big city before the border,
but there was still another seven to eight hundred kilometers to
the border. We went as usual to the local city hall, but this time
it was completely different. We waited for an hour before he let
us see him. This man was a peasant, he was even dressed like one,
when we told him our sad story he was staring at the ground,
then he slowly raised his head and said, "Do you know what a
mistake you people have done by coming all this way to Kunming from Shanghai? The border is very far away from here and
do you know that a lot of bridges have been exploded? And the
buses don't run regularly any more, you will have to walk most
of the way to the border, and I hear you have children, women,
and elderly people with you, how the hell do you people expect
to get there?" His face had turned red with anger. "You all have
given me unnecessary trouble, I have more important things to

solve, one thing is for sure I must get you people out of here as soon as possible. I need time, a day or so, to decide whether to send you back or to let you all to proceed to the border, please come tomorrow. By that time I think I will come up with a decision." When we reached our hotel as usual our elders asked us whether we had gotten permission to work, but when they saw our faces instantly they knew that we were in trouble, when we told them the story their morale fell even further, what was awaiting us tomorrow? We realized that we were in the hands of a cruel man, most probably he was a commie spy. This made us remember that many times we read in the local newspapers, that the commies somehow infiltrated to high government posts, from governor to general, we call them turncoats or traitors, that usually sold themselves to the commies and were ordered to play a double role. We learned later that such persons were liquidated by the same bosses who hired them, the commies. That night I hardly slept, and so did the others. I could hardly wait for the daybreak, when the time came to go we were all visibly nervous.

We arrived an hour early, we had to wait in a nearby café until the city hall opened. It was almost unbearable to wait. I had to control my nerves, so I decided to take a drink to calm my nerves. I asked for a drink but the coffee shop man did not sell hard drinks, so I had to go across the street to have one. I never drink in the morning, so the effect of the drink was almost instant, when I came to the others I felt much better, I even started to joke with the others just to try to bring their morale higher.

When we were allowed to enter his office he did not even bother to give us a "good day," just waved us to be seated. "You are very lucky," he said, "We made a reunion and decided to let you proceed with your journey. I warn you it will not be easy. Even our communications are sometimes interrupted with the interior of our province, so most of the time you will be on your own, these are rough times. The only thing we decided to help you with is to lend you a truck with a driver, to get you all as

24

near as possible to the border. You leave tomorrow at dawn." Without giving us a chance to say something he stood up and went away. We went to the hotel and decided to make our own reunion, to decide which family wanted to proceed the journey or wanted to go back to Shanghai. We called every one to a big hall in the hotel and told them the situation. My father, as the elder, proposed a democratic vote, and everybody agreed to do so. When every one settled down my father said in a loud voice, "Who wants to proceed, raise his right hand." To my surprise everyone raised his hand, including the children, imitating their parents.

So this is how we went to the unknown, this time what lay in front of us was jungle with small villages, but we knew that anything was better than falling in the hands of the commies.

My father knew them well from Russia, he was nearly shot there because he was trading horses. If not for a Gypsy commie official my father would have been killed. Yes there were also Gypsy communist officials in the Red Army, it's a matter of, if you cannot fight them join them.

Early next morning the truck arrived, it was an ordinary old truck which carried only cargo. Somehow we accommodated ourselves on the truck, using our baggage as seats, we were all excited because we did not know what awaited us in the near future. The very first day we had trouble with the truck, but the driver very quickly fixed it. The driver seemed to be a good man. I wanted to find out what his orders actually were, but he would not budge, he only said, "I was ordered to take you the border." We carried a lot of gas, so there was no worry about it. What worried me was the motor of the truck, it looked old and very tired. The road we traveled on was not bad, we found out later on that it was built by the US army, it was called General Stillwell's Highway. There were a lot of mountains in front of us. The going was very slow, because we were going up, the truck had a hard time pushing us up. Every now then we had to pour water in the old radiator, but then we ran out of water, so we had to stop by a creek to fetch water for the truck, or if not we had to walk for kilometers to find an isolated hut and ask for water. This took a lot of time and energy, but that day was good; we made about a hundred kilometers to the first village.

When we arrived we were met by the chief of the village, the driver showed him a piece of paper. We deduced it was from the Kunming mayor. He took us to a restaurant and said he would arrange for us to sleep right there in the restaurant, when the customers are gone, there were no hotels in the village. The owner arranged for the children and the elders a few beds, but the rest did what they could, I and my wife slept on the truck with some other couples, others put the tables together and used as a bed, the less fortunate slept on the ground, of course they used some sheets to spread on the ground and also to cover themselves. That night I shall never forget, my morale fell to such an extent that I silently cried. From Shanghai's luxury to a village in the middle of nowhere, sleeping on an old truck. I felt ashamed of myself and of my wife, thinking, "To what degree I have descended." The mosquitoes were king-size, although we were covered with a sheet the buzzing in the ear was terrible, I just could not shut an eye. The next morning we were up and ready to go but the damn truck would not start. He tried to fix it, but to no avail. He told us that another bus will pass and he will ask the other driver to do it, we waited for about four to five hours before the bus arrived.

I don't know how but he fixed it, but what disturbed us most was that the passengers were talking among themselves, something about an explosion. When my wife asked about it, nobody would say when or were the explosion occurred. I told my wife not to tell our elders about this rumor, but I think they sensed it, something was in the air but they did not know what. Anyway, we started to roll. We were somehow happy to be on the road again.

This time we arrived when the sun was beginning to set. The village was very small so the driver took us, to our surprise, to the army barracks. An officer came to the truck and talked to the driver, again the driver showed him the document, he nodded,

then came to inspect us. He then allowed us to ent
racks. He showed us where we could stay, it was a big
ordered some soldiers to bring some beds and a lot
The floor was wooden, so we all accommodated ourselves
better than the night before, only we were all hungry. The officer
said that there was no food left over to give us. He suggested for
us to buy our own food, but there was no ready food available,
so we had to buy raw food. We used their kitchen, it was almost
midnight before we had dinner. Then the officer told us something that scared the daylights out of us. He said that once you
leave the village it is already a communist territory. The outskirts
are all commies, the villages are still government-held. I did not
believe him, because I thought, why they did not stop us before
reaching this village? The answer to this question came the following day.

As we started our journey there was a huge mountain in
front of us. It was so steep that the truck hardly made thirty
kilometers an hour, it took us more than two hours to climb it.
I usually was sitting with the driver in front, but this time he
arranged a passenger, so I had to sit with the rest of my family
behind. The passenger was very well dressed, Chinese-style of
course, and he had a big handbag with him. When we began
to descend, all of a sudden we came to an abrupt stop. I must
explain to my reader that on the right side of the truck there was
a big abyss, going down for several kilometers. We even avoided
to see towards that angle because it seemed so dangerous. For a
minute or so we waited to see what happened, then we heard
voices from the forest on our left, I and some other youngsters
stood up to see what was going on. To our surprise about two
hundred meters from us the highway was not there, instead
there was a gap of about thirty meters missing.

At first we did not realize what was happening, but when I
saw our driver and the passenger come out of the cabin with their
hands high in the air, I knew that this was it, we were captured.
I told everybody to keep as quiet as possible, not to panic under
any circumstances. I told everyone to sit in their places and just

wait and see what happens. We heard a lot of talking in front of the truck. We were so tense that I even heard the footsteps coming towards us. An officer appeared. His uniform was a bit different of those of the government officers, the cap on his head that made a big difference, there was a big red star stamped on it. He spoke to us in a very educated tone, told us not to worry, that everything is under control. He asked us to descend from the truck and follow him. We wanted to take our things with us, but he told us not to take anything with us because we will return as soon as the road will be fixed. We had no choice. We could not argue with the commies. Besides, there was nobody working on the road. That made me feel that he was lying.

When we came to the edge of the road, there was a small track going up the mountain. The track was specially made for the partisans because it was made like a trench, it was waist high. Only one person could pass at a time. By this time there were a lot of them around us. Our driver was with us, but I could not see where our well-dressed passenger was. When he said we had to climb the mountain we were shocked. Our main problem was my father, a man at his age and almost a hundred and twenty kilos, how could he climb the mountain? But the officer insisted, he explained that it was for our own good. We asked him the reason why we had to do this, he told us that he will tell us when we reach the top of the mountain, he suggested we tie a rope around the waist of my father, put two young men in front of him, and pull the rope while other two would push him from behind. To our surprise it worked, but it was not easy. Every ten to fifteen minutes we had to stop to catch our breath. Amazingly my father did not look tired or stressed, maybe he controlled himself for our sake, not to have pity on him or something. Naturally we were accompanied by a Red soldier. When we reached the top our parents were sitting comfortably on the grass. I was very happy to see them. On the way up a lot of horrible things passed through my mind. After all, this was the first time we were captured by the commies. We had no idea what will happen to us so we were all very nervous. There were many soldiers with automatic rifles, including women, but very few were uniformed, the rest were all peasants. After a few hours of waiting my father asked my wife to look for the officer, and to ask him how long we will be held here. She went looking for him. I was still wondering where was the passenger that was with us. I started to walk just for curiosity. About a few hundred yards from where we were I saw the big bag which our passenger carried, but he was not in sight. Before long an officer came to the bag, called a soldier and told him to open it. He seemed to know what it contained. There were cartons of American cigarettes of many different brands. He emptied the bag on the ground and started to open the cartons, and then began to distribute the cigarettes to his officers and soldiers, then came over to us and also gave us a few packs.

When my wife came, we all gathered around her she said for us not worry, the officer in charge told her that the reason they brought us up here was for our own security, that only a few kilometers from here there was fighting going on with the government forces, and that we were headed right for the war area. That was the reason they exploded a piece of the highway, to prevent travel beyond that point, and also to prevent possible government reinforcement. About us, he said that as soon as he receives his orders he will fix the road and will let us proceed with our journey. We all were happy to hear the story, mostly because it made sense. If they went to so much trouble to hide us so that we would not get hurt, logically they would not harm us. Nevertheless we were told by our elders never to trust a commie. They even brought us food which was practically inedible. We could not refuse, so we had to push it down our throats to let them see that we were ordinary poor people, and eat everything that comes along.

After about an hour we heard a gunshot. Immediately there was a white streak of smoke in the sky, it was a signal. A few minutes later the officer came and told us that we could descend. "Shortly before you go away," said the officer, "I want you to listen to me for a few minutes. When you people reach your country, I would like you all to tell your people that we are liberating our country from the American capitalists and their puppets, Chiang Kai-shek regime, for they have robbed and corrupted our country for many years, and now it's up to us to clean the country from these blood-suckers. The war is a very cruel thing, many collaborators must be sacrificed, many innocent people will suffer, but this is the price we have to pay to make the revolution a success, it will take time before things will become normal again. You have done well for going home. There is nothing here now for you, go home and tell your people that China belongs to the Chinese and nobody else." Then he said, "The road is being fixed. When it's ready we will descend, and you shall continue your journey."

It was easy for others to descend, but not for my father. This time we still used the rope, but from behind. For me the trip was more dangerous, because if we should trip or something we could all go tumbling down the mountain, but thank God nothing went wrong. To show us his generosity, he ordered a couple of soldiers to help us unload our things, so that the truck would pass the damaged road unloaded. It was quite dangerous for the truck, it had to pass it with all the speed it contained, the only thing that helped because it was downhill. It was quite a suspense. We all held our breath when he rolled. The poor driver must have went through hell, but by a miracle he made it, then we all walked to the other side to him and gave him a big cheer. The officer waved us good bye and said, "Don't forget what I have told you," then we saw how they all went up the trail again. I saw how our elders made a sign of the cross on themselves, and even some murmured a prayer. For about five to six kilometers there was no evidence of a recent battle, then someone pointed and said, "Over there." We all stood up to see, there was black smoke and some trees on fire, a little further we saw some dead bodies scattered around. We quickly sat down and did not dare to look again. So the officer did not lie, there was a battle, but nobody knew who won it.

We arrived at the village a few hours later, we were met by government soldiers armed up to the teeth. They seemed very nervous, that made me think that they must have lost the battle. We were a burden and we knew it, who needed refugees under such circumstances? But we were there, they had to accommodate us. We did not dare to ask for any kind of help, we went and bought our own food and somehow managed to pass that night, but I am sure that very few of us had shut an eye. It was still dark when I went to the driver and woke him up, but he got angry and said he would not travel in darkness. It was very dangerous, besides the soldiers won't let us pass till the sun gets higher. We did not even eat anything, we only gave some bread to the children, we could not wait to buy milk or something, our thoughts was to get out of the village as soon as possible.

We did not know it then, but this was to be the last time we traveled by this truck, because the next village we came to, there was a big bridge crossing a river, the bridge was almost destroyed. The local peasants lined up some wooden planks on the bridge so that you could cross it by foot. So this was it, from here on we had to walk. On top of all this misfortune we were completely out of local money.

I don't remember who, but someone had an idea to try and sell our personal clothing, so we opened our suitcases. Immediately there was a crowd gathered around us. I had a lot of good suits and shirts, but to our surprise they were not interested in a whole suit, or a shirt or any other item, all they wanted was the waistcoats, and they paid a good price for them. I remember we sold a lot of them. Another thing I noticed that these Chinese peasants were from another tribe, their faces were different, they spoke among themselves in a different dialect, and we were only a couple of hundred kilometers from Kunming.

We sadly said farewell to our driver, after all he helped us a lot and we all thanked him for that. To cross the bridge we had a problem, it was dangerous for a normal man to cross it, imagine my father. The wooden planks were very thin. You had to cross it step by step, the river below was very rough, there were no boats to take anyone across, so there was only one way. The bridge was twelve feet wide and about thirty feet long, the wooden planks were sometimes not connected with each other, so you had to make a wide step to get to the other plank. You had to have a lot of balance, otherwise you were a cooked duck. The height between the bridge and the river was about fifty feet, so you just can imagine what we went through. There is no way to describe our faces when we started to cross that confounded bridge, it was as if we were on our way to a Nazi gas chamber, we held each other by our hands, and then only God led us to the other side.

There were a few shops and some huts who sold food and drinks. I personally needed a drink, so I went as fast as I could to the hut to buy me one. When I got there I was not the only one with the idea, almost half of the clan was there having a drink. We had money to spend so some of us, including me, exaggerated a little, and before long someone got a guitar and we started to sing a song. That made the natives come closer to us, and gazed at us as if we were from Mars. When we finished singing, they started singing their own songs. It did not sound like Chinese, but something like African sounds.

Now we were by foot we had to face the facts, on top of all this, we had, to be exact, three pregnant women, four to five children under ten years, or a little bit older, we had over four hundred kilometers to go, not to mention the elders. We had quite a problem to solve. Again we made a reunion, this time it took us two to three hours to come to a decision, some wanted to return and face the music, others wanted to continue the journey, but the majority wanted to leave China for good. We decided to start working even in the villages, and try to sell every thing we had. We saw a lot of horses and donkeys in the village, so we decided to hire some to carry the children and some of our elders. We had a hard time convincing the owners of the horses and the donkeys to hire them to us, they wanted us to buy them but we had no money for such a transaction. Somehow they agreed to take us as far as three villages towards the border. First of all we accommodated the pregnant women and children on the donkeys. The elders used the horses. We found for my father a working horse, that they usually use for extra hard work, yet the horse could hardly carry him. My father loved it because it reminded him of his youth in Russia, it's been decades since he mounted a horse. For us youngsters the walking on the road was an adventure, with all that jungle around us, with all those wild animals, like all different types of birds, and even monkeys jumping from one tree to another. This was already a tropical area, it was very hot, but we youngsters did not feel it, but our elders suffered from the heat.

I estimated we averaged twenty to twenty five kilometers per day, it also depended how far the village was one from another, we had to arrive before sunset. The next village we arrived was a little larger then the one we came from. The officer in charge received us well. He even offered us food. In return of his generosity we told him that we will put on a show for him and his soldiers, and so we did right in the middle of the barracks. After the show, to our surprise, the officer started to collect money for us from his soldiers. This was exactly what we intended to do in the future, give shows in barracks and invite civilians if possible, this picked up our morale. Since the officer was a good man, we asked him if he could give us a recommendation for the next village; he promptly obliged. I was surprised of the amount of money we collected. By the way, the money by now were all in silver coins, the smallest was a twenty-five cent coin, the biggest was a Chinese dollar coin, which was called tatoo or showtoo, which means big head or small head because of the heads stamped on the coin. No paper money were accepted. The coins were of pure silver and dated a century ago. Up 'til now I regret that I did not bring with me some of those coins. Collectors of other countries could have paid a lot of money for them, but who thought of collecting anything, our only thought was to get out of China as soon as possible, and be in a city like Shanghai, China, was or even half as Shanghai. All my life I was in a city, and now in the middle of a jungle that seemed like it will never end, and not knowing what will happen to us a day from now.

Once the village was further then it usually is from other villages, and the sun was setting real fast. The owner of the horses, also serving as guide, told us to hurry. He said that there was a hut and a stable just a few hundred meters away, and that he will ask the owner to let us sleep in the stable, for a price of course. When we arrived, the owner met us with a rifle in his hand, but soon relaxed when he saw that we were strangers with children and women. He readily agreed to let us use the barn. We all hurried in to try and get the best places. My wife and I usually stayed behind. We did not like to dispute places, any place was good for us. There were two horses sharing the stable with us. Of course the owner took the horses deep inside the stable, and tied them up there for them not to bother us. There was a lot of hay, and he told us to help ourselves to it, so everybody started to spread the hay on the ground as much as possible. It was getting dark very fast. He brought us a bowl which contained a little oil, and a very thin cotton string. He took a match and put fire to it, then he put it right in the middle of the stable, that was to illuminate the night for us, but I knew that the oil will last for a couple of hours or so. I spread the hay right opposite the stable door, the rest were all on the other side of me, so I and my wife were the only ones separated from all the rest. He also brought us few pieces of wood to make fire, not that it was cold, but just to make the stable look brighter. The light in the stable did not last long. It was pitch dark, except for the embers of the fire, which was very dim.

It was way past midnight when I heard something outside the door of the stable. I was not the only one who heard the sound, my mother was a very light sleeper, and so were others, but nobody made a sound, my mother promptly assured me that there must be a small animal trying to get into the stable. She said that of course to calm me and the others who did not sleep, but when there was a knock on the door, and a sound that I could not distinguish, it was not a animal's sound, neither it was a human sound, it sounded something out of this world. The banging on the door became louder all the time, the sound, later a scream, sounded horrible. By this time almost every one was wide awake, but nobody uttered a word. My mother only said, "Don't be afraid, my son, keep calm, there must be an explanation." Just after she finished her words, the door burst open, somebody or something started to come towards me. I was completely paralyzed by fear, and so was my wife. She was behind me and hugging me with all her strength. The thing was coming towards me slowly and making funny sounds. I immediately released myself from my wife's hug, and slowly stood up to face the thing. I needed to protect myself under any circumstances. As I said, I could not see an inch from my nose. I decided to attack first, don't ask me why, because 'til this day I don't know why. I did not know I had this hidden ability in me. When this thing came so near that I could hear him breathe, I leaped on it with all my might. To my surprise I hit something small. I was on top of what seemed to me a little man. I said, "I got him," with a loud voice. By this time about ten to fifteen of us had match sticks burning in their hands. It was a little boy. To my relief he seemed more frightened than we were. I spoke to him, but he would not answer, for the simple reason that he was deaf and dumb. That explained the sounds he made at the door. It seems that the stable was his house, and we invaded it.

The going from there on was rough because the highway was going upwards, and the villages were every time further from each other, but once we reached a village we always gave a show, if not for money, only for food and shelter. The peasants were completely changing their form, I mean physically. They looked not like Chinese but some what darker, the further we went the darker they got. Only the authorities spoke the official Chinese language, the peasants spoke a completely different dialect.

One day we started a little late our journey, an hour or so before sunset we had to get off the main road, to get to a place were we could overnight. When we got there the whole village ran away, they thought that we were some kind of enemies that came to kill them. Our guide told us to wait outside the village. It took him at least twenty minutes to convince them that we were no enemies, but people like them in distress, then slowly by slowly they began to return, but more for curiosity, some of them have never seen white people in their lives. They were dressed completely different from the Chinese we know, their women had a lot of metal rings around their necks, that reminded me of some African women that I saw in some cinema, I cannot recall which one, who wore the same type rings. I must have thought to myself, two countries so different and so far away from each other, and still had something in common, this might prove that the origin of mankind is from the same tree.

I have mentioned that three of our women were pregnant, two of them were my sisters, the husband of one of my sisters calculated that my sister would give birth within a week or ten days, the other two were also within this range. This was a problem, our only chance was to get to a larger village in time. One thing was good, that all three of them were already mothers, but the other children were all born in first-class hospitals, now it seems the elder women will have to take over, and even they have no experience, but the last big village before the border was a couple of hundred kilometers away, only God knows how will they make it. But God is good, a beautiful girl was born to my sister just a hundred and fifty kilometers from the border. The village was not too big, there was no doctors, but a local peasant woman came to help and every thing went fine. These last hundred and fifty kilometers were the hardest to make, partly because it was almost uphill, and also the villages were too small to give shows. We could not afford to hire animals and guides anymore, so we were on our own. Who suffered most, of course the pregnant women and the elders, but before we arrived on the border, the other two women gave birth a week or so apart from each other.

When we arrived on the border we were met by a high ranking officer. To our dismay, he told us that a day before some red-leaning Burmese rebels occupied the village on their side of the border, so it was officially closed. Nobody could cross to the other side because the Chinese border was still government-held. We were all shocked. We were so near and yet so far. We knew that either side must change for us to cross the border, and the high-ranking officer confirmed it, but he assured us that it will not take long before the border opens, and that all expenses for hotel and food will be paid by him, providing we make a show for his officers and soldiers. He seemed to be like a good fellow. He invited us for dinner, of course only the four of us who were in charge to promote the show.

There was no theater or any kind of hall, the barracks were out of bounds, so where could we perform? He came up with an idea. He said he had a lot of empty gasoline barrels, put some wooden planks on them, cover them with a canvas, and so we had a stage. To change our costumes he would mount a tent just behind the stage. I remember that it was a few days before New Year's Eve, that is, 1949 to 1950. The next day we gave our performance. He liked it so much that he invited all of us to the New Year's party. Besides the good food we even had American whiskey and beer at our disposal, we all had quite a ball, we all had a little more than necessary to drink, and the party went on 'til the little hours of the morning.

Performance on the China-Burma border, January 1950, the author on the accordion, his sister Lida dancing. (Courtesy of the author.)

The big surprise came to us that very morning. I was still sleeping when someone woke me up, and told me to come out and see what's happening. When I came out everyone was looking up towards the army headquarters I automatically looked up. I almost collapsed. The flag on the mast was red with yellow stars in the corner of it. It was the first time I saw a Chinese communist flag. After what seemed to be an eternity we saw our high official come out of the barracks with a completely different uniform, and the famous cap with the red star on it. He came up to us and said, "Did I not promise to you all that you shall cross the border soon, so this is it. You can all cross the border now, because both sides are communist." On the other side was just a small group of communist rebels, but the Burmese government was democratic, free from communism.

Within a half an hour we were on the other side, all we had to do is cross a small bridge that divided the two countries. I turned to look behind and amazingly tears came to my eyes. After all I was born there, and my teen-age fun and friends were left behind forever. We crossed the border without an incident. By now we practically had no language. On the way we sold everything, some heavy things which we could not sell we left behind. When we hit the road some were crying, some were singing, others were laughing, we made it. Although we still had a lot to go, our morale was high. We were in a different country, the road to freedom, this was what made us happy and gave us stamina to go on.

We were just a few hours on the road, when out of nowhere Burmese troops appeared. Their uniforms were identical to British soldiers'. We were not surprised. We knew that Burma was once a British colony. The officer in charge gave us a salute and spoke to us in fluent English. "You must be refugees," he said. The first thing he did was distribute army food rations, very similar to the American rations, then he asked us if the border village was still occupied by the Red rebels. We said yes. "How many rebels do you think were in the village?" We said we did not know exactly, but he insisted and said, approximately. We talked among ourselves and came to a number not very accurate, so we decided to tell him that there were about fifty to sixty rebels. He thanked us very warmly and said, "You all have been a big help." The first town was only thirty kilometers from here, by the name of Maymyo, he also assured us that there was an Anglo-Indian colony there, which surely will help us with all our needs.

We made those thirty kilometers in record time. We were met by the local authorities at the edge of the town; they must have been alerted by the officer by radio. For the first time in months we saw decently-dressed people, that made us feel that civilization was near. They treated us very well, and almost immediately offered us to perform for them in their club as soon as possible. They accommodated us in a small but comfortable guest house. Compared to what we were used to, this was Paradise. Things began to look up for us. The food they offered was European and it tasted excellent. This time the show was completely spoken in English. My cousin Jerry was the man who commanded the jokes, and he was very funny too. 'Til today I don't know were he managed to have so many jokes hidden up his sleeve. This time he enjoyed himself very much, because the audience understood every word he said, and they rolled over with laughter. Here he was the star of the show, and he loved it. But as the town was small, we managed to give three shows only.

We had to continue our journey, but this time by train, the next town was Lashio. Here we also gave a few shows, but here something different happened, my sister's only daughter, by the name of Zina, found her self a boy friend. She was only 13 years old, but already built as an adult woman, and very beautiful. He was a son of an Englishman and his mother was Indian. When we were all getting prepared to leave to a city called Mandalay, the second biggest city of Burma, she eloped with him. This was a terrible shock to my sister and to all of us. When we arrived in Mandalay, we went to the police. We made a complaint that our girl was stolen from us. Of course at that time we did not know that she willingly eloped with him. Now we were on our own. Nobody thought of giving shows, our thoughts were how to get our girl back. For money we used our dollars, you could change in the banks any amount you wanted to. The local police naturally were on the side of their citizen, after all he was Burmese by birth, so they took the case very lightly. They promised they would search for them, but a week passed and nothing happened. My sister and her husband practically slept in the police station. We even went to see the governor, but he refused to see us, there was no consulates of any country in Mandalay, the nearest consulates were in Rangoon, Burma, the capital of the country.

It took three days by boat to reach the capital. To impress the governor we said we out of money, and as refugees it was their responsibility to take care of us. The police stalled, or maybe they really did not know where they were. By this time we were moved to a big guest house, enough to accommodate all of us. For food the Islamic community provided us with it, as we were Iranian citizens.

I must explain that my grandparents were born in Iran, then evacuated to Russia and then to China, it is not like in Brazil, that if you are born in Brazil, you must be Brazilian. If I was born in a stable that does not mean that I am a horse!

They felt that they should help, the saying says Muslim should help a Muslim under any circumstances, but what they did not know that we were all Catholics. We thanked them anyway for their generosity.

We had some trouble with the local Anglo-Indians. Once the father of the missing girl, and few of our other elders, were in a bar having a drink, when some Anglo- Indians entered in the bar, after a few drinks they started to ask if we found our girl and making jokes out of it. That irritated our elders. They had no choice but to start a fight. They completely destroyed the bar. One of ours and two of theirs were taken to the hospital. One of theirs was gravely hurt, but thank God nobody died.

For security reasons our guest house was surrounded by the police. The officer said that we might be attacked by local Anglo-Indian hooligans for revenge. We decided to send a telegram to the Rangoon foreign office, and related our situation. The answer was for us to leave to Rangoon immediately. The officer in charge of us was furious, because we went over his head and contacted Rangoon without letting him know. He must have got hell from his superiors. He told us to get ready to leave for Rangoon the next morning, but we did not budge. We wanted our girl with us. Even the highest official of the police came to convince us to travel, but we all said no. When they saw that we were serious about the situation, two days later they found her, but in vain. Just as we were getting ready to leave she managed to run away again. This made things change. My sister and her husband decided that from Rangoon, Burma, the authorities might be more sympathetic to our cause. Besides, there must be some authority representing Iranian affairs, so Zina was left behind with her Anglo-Indian lover.

By the way, his name was Robin Davidson. He also had a brother, his name was Mikey. I mentioned him in my story because I have a good reason to do so, later in this story the reader will find out why.

We traveled to Rangoon by the Irrawaddy river. It took us three days to arrive in the capital. As usual we were met by the local authorities. They treated us very well and took us outside of town to a big empty house. To our surprise it was all fixed up to receive us. It was not bad. Each family had its own privacy. There were beds and even some furniture. They gave every family some money according to their needs, and there was already a lot of army rations piled up in the store room. They said all this was courtesy of the government, the money were to be used for fresh vegetables, cigarettes, and other expenses. Meanwhile we had to wait 'til the authorities decide what to do with us.

Our first protest was of course about Zina, we wanted her here under any circumstances, they promised that they will work on the problem as soon as possible. That did not satisfy my sister. She found out that the Indian Embassy was who took care of Iranian affairs, so she quickly went to the Embassy to complain about the situation of her daughter. He already knew about the situation and said that Zina was to blame because she did not want to come home to her mother, and that she loved the boy and would get married to him, he could not take her by force, the Burmese authorities would not allow. My sister came home crying like a baby. Her husband, as usual, got drunk and wanted to pick a fight with any Indian that came along. Of course we did not let him do that.

Later the consulate came to inform us that he had sent a wire to our consulate in India and informed them of our situation, and that he was awaiting a reply. It took a long while before it came. It said that they also sent a wire to Iran, to ask what to do with us. It seems that Iran had no experience to deal with refugees, so it will take time before they come to a decision. And on top of all that, the house we were in was supposedly haunted, it was an ex-Japanese torture house, and many people were killed there, that's what our neighbors told us. After that nobody dared to go out alone at night, including me, naturally some of us claimed to have seen something unusual, but I personally did not see anything. There was a room beneath the house which was very dirty, and there was stains on the walls, what seemed to be blood, some of us took it very seriously, and even wanted to move from there, but nobody dared to stay away from each other. Actually Rangoon, Burma, is a big city, after Shanghai this was the biggest city we saw up 'til now. So naturally the youngsters, including me, used to go out Saturdays to paint the town red. We gave a lot of trouble to the local police, there were lots of fights in bars or nightclubs. Generally my people are not violent, but the thought of losing our Zina to these bastards, we must have generated this violence in us, we somehow blamed the whole country for what they did to us. I know we were wrong, but when you are young you look at things differently. We did these things so frequently that the police decided to keep us in the house, and only let us go to buy things escorted. We were virtually prisoners. But we always found a way to run away on our own, and came back usually the next day, as if nothing had happened, unless we had a fight and had to be taken out of jail by our Indian consul. The whole town knew us and were somewhat afraid of us, that made us feel good, revenge sometimes is sweet.

It took a couple of months before the Iranian authorities decided to act—by this time we were sick and tired of waiting—when the Indian consul came and told us that he received orders to buy us tickets to Calcutta, India, and from then on the Iranian consul will take over. He visibly seemed relieved to get rid of us, after so much trouble we gave him. But then came a shock. My auntie's husband and his brother were English subjects, they were born in Hong Kong, and other two families were stateless. That excluded them from the trip to India. My auntie and her children were Iranian subjects, but she could not let her husband behind, so for the first time we had to be separated. I will never forget the day we had to leave. When the bus arrived to take us to the ship there was a lot of crying and screaming, hugging each other, as if we were all going away forever. We

Gypsies are very sentimental about such conditions, we were all practically related to each other, and that hurt a lot. After all, we have been together all our lives, and now God knows when we will see each other again.

The trip to Calcutta, India, was about a week or so, there was only one stop. It was Decca, East Pakistan; that does not exist anymore, today it is Bangladesh. The food on the ship was bad. We traveled third class, that was the reason why the food was horrible, so we had to go ashore in Decca to buy some decent food.

At last we arrived in Calcutta. On the dock our Iranian consul was waiting for us. To his surprise we did not know a word of Iranian, but he spoke very well in English. He immediately took us to a Iranian-owned pension. The owners of the pension were also Iranian-born, but they were Armenians, and were Iranian subjects like us. They greeted us very warmly. As we were preparing to settle down the press appeared. They started to ask a lot of questions from our elders. Of course, I avoided the press and went to my room. I was to tired for conversation. All I wanted was to have dinner and go to bed.

When the press left we were invited to have dinner. At the table we were served by a beautiful young girl, she was the owner's daughter. Later I was told her name was Cynthia. Although she knew that I was married, I had the feeling that every time she served me she gave me that famous look, or was it my impression? Later on I discovered that it was not my impression, she fell for me like a ton of bricks.

Calcutta was a city something like Shanghai, so we had no hurry to leave the city, all we needed to find a nightclub so we could work, and there were hundreds of them. Surely we could find one for us to work, but the problem was our consul. He wanted us to travel to Iran as soon as possible.

The press gave us the front page, with photos of our elders all over it. Of course, as usual the press exaggerated. They even wrote that we were tortured, our women raped, and that one was stolen and may be killed by now, and that the United Nations will take the case, and give a strong protest to Communist China for treating refugees in such a manner.

My sisters quickly found work in one of the biggest nightclubs. I was included as a musician. The rest found work as salesmen or musicians in other nightclubs. It was easy. The consulate paid our food and board, the money we made was all profit. Actually we were not allowed to work officially, we were in transit to our country, but who cared? The Indian authorities were sympathetic to our condition—it must have been the press that helped us a lot—so they just pretended not to see what we were doing. But the consul was on our neck After a month or so he said that he has spent the money that the Iranian government has sent us, and if we would not leave at once he would stop paying our food and board. But after all we did not know what awaited us in Iran.

I personally liked it here, we had a big Chinatown. We already made good friends, and also made business with the Chinese, selling imported Chinese articles to our foreign friends, some times even jewelry brought from Tibet. I made a lot of money on such transactions. Because of the invasion of the Chinese of Tibet, the refugees from there who were rich sold their jewelry for almost half the price. I sometimes had to go to up north to Darjeeling, India, to buy the jewelry first hand.

Besides, Cynthia was at hand and I was flirting with her secretly. But the poor girl took me for granted, and wanted to marry me under any circumstances, this sort of thing comes in the open some time. When my wife found out she went to her house and made a scandal. To a girl of her age this was a tremendous shock. She did not think twice. She bought some sleeping pills and nearly killed herself. If her brother would not have found her in the bathroom collapsed on the floor, she would have been dead by now. Still, her father called the police, and I had to accompany them to the police station to sign a certificate that I will not molest her any more or even talk to her again. If I will break my treaty I would immediately be deported from India.

My middle sister, also named Zina, was left behind in China, she was married to a White Russian. We got a telegram from her that she was arriving in Calcutta. We were all happy to hear this wonderful news. When she came to our hotel she was alone. Her husband was stateless and was not allowed to accompany her.

She told weird stories about how the communists treated the foreigners in Shanghai. They all were gathered into camps. Men and women were separated. Anyone that had the slightest case with the police with the other government, was rearrested and given a trial again. But those who worked for the other government were prosecuted and given big sentences. These people were sent to prison. Many died there, some crippled by torture, some went mad from daily interrogations, those who survived were mostly brainwashed, they were send back to the camp to try and convince the others that the communist system was the best thing for the world. If not for the help of the American-run IRO organization, even in the camp the people would have died of hunger. We considered ourselves lucky that we made it just in time.

My sister could not believe her eyes when she saw so much food in the markets and shops, it took a lot of time for her to come to, slowly by slowly she became normal again.

By now we were two years in India. The consul was furious with us. Somehow he persuaded the Indian authorities to give us orders to leave the country. We did all in our power to stay, but to no avail, so we were transferred from Calcutta to Bombay, India, to catch a ship to Iran. We had to wait a week or so for the ship. Meanwhile we received a letter from our people who we left behind, that two families crossed the border to India from Burma clandestinely. I don't know how they did it. They were all well and asked us for some addresses of the people we worked with in Calcutta so they can continue the work we did not need.

Now we were off to the unknown, to Iran, which was our country only by the documents. I went to the library and asked for books about Iran. What I found in the books I did not like, the country was small, very poor and Islamic. Christians were not respected to much, and for us to find jobs was difficult, particularly musicians. But there was one hope, there were a lot of different nationalities in the capital which is called Tehran. There were Russians, Armenians, and Syrians, which I thought will be some help to do business with.

And so the ship arrived. It was a small ship, about 3000 thousand tons, and it was a British-owned liner, her name was Dara. As we were considered Europeans by the British, we were given second-class accommodations. Our first stop was Pakistan, the capital is Karachi, and is a very big city but not too clean. We stayed there for three days to unload and load cargo, so we had time enough to see the city.

Before I go any further I would like to remind my reader that I promised to explain our Gypsy origin in the earlier stages of this book, of course, in my opinion. In the two years that I lived in India I learned to believe that we Gypsies are from there and nowhere else. I will try to explain why. For example their language is very similar to ours, in some cases exactly like ours. For instance they count from one to ten exactly like we do, and I mean all Gypsy tribes without exception. There are hundred of words they use as we do, like eyes, hair, lips, ears, mouth, far, old, etc., etc. And also, while traveling from Calcutta to Bombay our train stopped at railway station. My father and the rest of our people were astonished to see that the women were dressed the same way like our women were dressed in Russia a century ago.

My father and other elders confirmed my belief. Very recently Indira Gandhi when she still was the prime minister of India, she assembled about ten to fifteen different tribes of Gypsies, musicians singers and dancers from all over the world, including Russian Gypsies who by chance were our far relatives. When I visited them in Stockholm Sweden, they showed me a videotape of the show they performed in India. The prime minister, Indira Gandhi, talked to my people and confirmed that we were from her country. How I saw my people in Stockholm I will relate later in this book.

In Karachi I visited a few Muslim shrines, went to the cinema, tasted the local food, took some photographs and that was all. As a matter of fact my hobby was to take photographs of different countries I visited; I still have them till today. Our next stop was Musqat, right at the mouth of the Persian Gulf. We even did not go ashore because it was so small, nevertheless I was curious to see it because it was the first Arabian port. The food on the ship was typically British, oxtail soup, then came fried fish with some boiled potatoes. The main dish was usually beef steak with some vegetables. The steak was so thin that the fan which was blowing could blow it off the dish, so we were obliged to buy some food in the canteen. Other wise we all would have been on a diet.

This ship had other sister ships by the names of Daresa and Dumra, they made the trip Bombay to Basra, Iraq, stopping at Musqat, Dubai, Bahrein, Kuwait, these are all small Arab sheikdoms. Then comes Iran. You enter the river Karun, you bypass the city of Abadan, the biggest oil refinery in the region, then you arrive at Khorramshahr, that was our destination. The river was divided in two, on your left was Iraq, on your right, Iran.

The moment we entered the river we could see the poorness of both countries, the houses were made of mud. I personally felt like I was back in the Chinese jungle that we have passed. My mother begun to cry, I remember she told me, "My son, here we will suffer." I tried to comfort her, and I said to her, "Mother, we have gone through worse situations, don't worry, we will manage, we always did." Then I turned around and saw the faces of my people, they were all serious with that angry look in their eyes. Then someone said, "My God, this country looks like it is a hundred years behind our time." It could not be compared to Shanghai, or even Calcutta. All our lives we lived in a big city, no wonder they were so upset, we had nothing to do but face the music. Besides all this misfortune, the temperature was as high as 46 centigrade, we never in our lives faced such temperatures. When we asked an officer of the ship if the weather was normal at such temperatures he said that it even goes higher, up to 50 to 52, but he quickly tried to calm us down, by saying that in the capital, the temperature there is half this much because Tehran is over two thousand feet high. I was afraid that my father and the other elders could not support this heat, the solution was to get them out of Khorramshahr as soon as possible and we did just that.

Right from the docks we went to the railway station, we had to wait for about four hours to catch the train to Tehran, the capital of Iran. When we finally got on the train there was a sense of relief to all of us. After a few hours of traveling we felt that the air was getting cooler, because we were going upwards all the time. I have never seen a railroad line so complicated, we passed over fifty tunnels, snaking from one to another dangerously, but we did not mind, getting from the heat was our objective.

When we arrived in Tehran, we became a little more optimistic because of the size of the city. It was not as big as other capitals. It had European style buildings. Later we found out the railroad that brought us here, and the city, was built by German engineers. The father of the King Reza Pahlavi was said to be very fond of German technology, and also a strong ally of Germany. That cost him his life. But that is another story.

In Tehran was a different story, we came to our destination so every family was on its own. We did not live even in the same hotels. Within a week of our arrival the foreign office asked us to come to their headquarters. They started to ask us serious political questions. The reader must understand that this country was a kingdom, and were terrified of communist infiltration. So one by one we were questioned. I don't blame them. After all we were from a communist country, and lived there for most of our lives. They asked me if the commies brainwashed me, I told them I would not be here if they did. They were very gentle and did not accuse us of anything, but warned us to stay out of politics.

Then they changed the subject and asked what work we are going to do. We told them will go to the local Russian club and talk to their leaders, ask them to help us where we could invest our money that we earned in India, and also find jobs for our young people. They did not ask us how much money we had, they seemed satisfied with our answers. My sisters were first to find a job in foreign nightclubs. There were very few, but they were filled with Americans. The clubs needed singers who sang in English, musicians were scarce who played English music, so for my family and few other musicians it was wonderful, the pay was more than good and the fun was even better. I always loved music and it was good to be in show business again. At that time there was a organization called the Point Four, it was of course American. I cannot say exactly what their function was, and I did not care as long as they provided work for us. They were all dressed in civilian clothes, but later on we knew that they were military. After they opened up the NCO club, we used to work there only when they had parties during the day, there they used their uniforms, they were very generous with their tips.

By this time a telegram came from my sister's daughter already with a child, and stated that she wanted to join us, so my family decided to go and get her, and also see our people who were left behind. We went back the same way we came, only we did not go up 'til Burma. Only my sister and her husband went up to Mandalay to get her. Meanwhile in India we were very happy to see our relatives again, they were working with the people we indicated for them, and they thanked us a lot for it. This time we began to work with them until my sister arrived with her daughter and her daughter's husband, Robin Davidson.

Again we overstayed. Our visa was only for three months, so we had to pay a fine and apply again for an extension.

Some of our contacts with whom we made business had moved to Bombay, so we had to follow them, only this time the work we had to do was a little outside the law. At that time Bombay was dry, it means that liquor was completely prohibited, but only a few hours ride from Bombay, there was a Portuguese colony, by the name of Goa, which was a free port. You could buy from a needle to a diamond for half the price, including liquor. As we were foreigners we were allowed to bring from Goa four bottles of whisky or any other type of liquor. In India this was worth its weight in gold, so we used to go up and down at least ten days in a month, and bring the liquor, including my cousins, and there were a lot of them. Business was so good that I decided to transfer my father to Goa, so that he may buy the liquor for us, so we could come and just pick it up, and also it was very cheap to live in Goa than in Bombay.

But as I said before, war was always one step behind of me. India declared that they wanted their land back. I did not know it then that this dispute was going on a long time, only this time they blocked off Goa completely, and brought their army in, and said they would invade Goa unless the Portuguese would not leave peacefully. So I was separated from my parents. I was in Bombay, and they were in Goa with some of my cousins. Of course the dispute between the two countries was so serious that the United Nations stepped in to try and stop a possible bloodshed.

Meanwhile we had to wait for the outcome, and this situation changed my life. To start with, I was out of work, lonely, depressed mentally and physically, I thought I would never see my parents again. My wife was no help to me, she could not give me a child, we went to lot of doctors to no avail. So deep inside of me I secretly prayed to God that I could separate from her and marry somebody of my race, but there were no young girls available. So I decided to go out and have some fun and try to forget my sorrows, and this was exactly what I did. I found a billiard hall and walked in. I was good at it in China, I was curious to see if I still could play as I did there. I met two Anglo-Indian boys. I practically forced myself on them, but they did not mind. I think they sensed that I needed company and badly, so they accepted me as a friend. When it got dark I invited them for dinner. On the way I asked them where we could buy some local liquor. I knew that imported liquor was very expensive for us, to my surprise one of them said that there is an Iranian restaurant that sells liquor, but actually, they tried to explain, that it is a medicine sold at pharmacies especially for pregnant women, its pure alcohol mixed with some vitamins usually given to women after giving birth. When you mix it with Coca-Cola the taste is exactly like whisky Coke. The only trouble was that when you got high on it you stay high from two to three hours, and the hangover is terrible, it was called among my new-found friends the Stringer. There I got acquainted to their clan. There were many Anglo-Indian girls, but one in particular attracted my attention. Her name was Rita White, she was about my age and married, but her husband was in England, and I was told that he was at least twenty years older than she was. My wife got sick with some unknown fever. She had to go the hospital. It was not a serious sickness so I was not worried. In the meantime, I went out with the clan almost every night. I had money to spend, and besides I liked Rita a lot, she made me forget my troubles real fast, that was exactly the medicine I needed at that time. I did not know it then but, this was the beginning and the end of my marriage. Oh, yes, I had a lot of fun with that clan, this is one part of my life I shall never forget, because it marked the second and the most important thing in my life, my second marriage. No it was not Rita, but someone that was always near to me and even my relative, but this will come a little later in my story.

When finally my father and the rest arrived from Goa, we were obliged to leave for Iran almost immediately. The Indian foreign office would not extend our visas, so again we had to go back to Iran the same way we came, but as far as I am concerned this time it was my destiny to a happier life.

In Iran we got back our old jobs, but this time not only for the Americans but also for other private clubs, even foreign embassies, etc., etc. My wife was somewhat uneasy with me, she sensed that I was getting cooler towards her, and also I began to spend more time with my musician friends than with her, so she went her way and I went mine. Although we were still together, it was just a matter of time for our separation.

Then Lady Luck came my way, because my auntie came to join us in Iran from India. She had twin daughters who were almost my age, she had also two granddaughters which her son gave her to raise, because the mother of the girls died young, and he married again, surprisingly to my sister Lida, who I have mentioned earlier that she was the star of the show. He was my first cousin as well as my sister's. His two little girls were very young when I saw them last, one was ten years old, the elder was twelve, almost three years passed since we were together. When someone told me that they were in Tehran, I naturally went to see them. I cannot explain my surprise when I saw the elder daughter of my cousin. She was a beautiful grown-up woman, her beauty the typical Gypsy type, the color of her skin was as if tanned by the sun, her eyes brown which had a brilliant glow, which could be seen even in the dark, this was what I was waiting for. I fell for her like a million tons of bricks, now the question was, will she have at least half of the feelings that I had for her? After all I was eight years older than her, and besides I was still married officially. She did not know what was going on between me and my wife. When we went to visit them my wife was also with me. Instantly she noticed how I looked at Maita, that is her name in Gypsy, but she is called Margarita in any language. I remember my wife told me when we were at home, "Now I know that I lost you for forever to this Maita, for she is Gypsy and your relative. From foreign girls I was not afraid that you could leave me, but to this girl I lost you forever, so if you want a new start for us don't ever see this girl again." I did not answer her that night, the only thing on my mind was Maita. I had to find a way to visit her more often than actually permitted, I was afraid that my auntie would not get suspicious, so I had to have a trick up my sleeve. It took me a day or so to come up with one.

I knew that my auntie was very fond of bingo, so I went and bought the game and gave her as a present. Naturally now I could visit her any time so we could play the game together, slowly by slowly my auntie got used to my frequent visits. In the meantime my wife was good to her word, one day she just left me without giving me notice. For the first time in my life I felt a sense of relief. I must admit that I had some feelings for her at some time of my marriage, but when I saw Maita, I became immune to whatever was left of my feelings for my wife. Maita knew very well that I was after her, but she did not give way 'til my wife was gone. Then one day I was invited to a Russian party and so was Maita, and her twin aunties, of course. I was very happy to see them there. That was the first time I asked her to dance with me. When I held her in my arms and pressed her body towards mine I could feel her trembling, then she said softly, "So your wife has left you." I quickly answered, "It is you to blame, she knew that I am in love with you." The twins were already suspicious that I was courting Maita, but on our way back to home on the taxi I could not resist not to kiss Maita right on her lips, in front of her twin aunties. That confirmed our relationship. The trouble was that one of the twins, Neni to be exact, was against this romance, for some reason or another, but the other, Lola, was not. This I found out later because in front of me they did not dare to show their feelings. From here on I had to meet secretly with Maita, but mostly during the day. My family knew of my intentions, it went so far that my elder sister told me not to spoil Maita unless I had serious plans, after all she was my cousin's daughter, and also my other sister's husband Lida. I was afraid that if I marry Maita my cousin would leave my sister, which they had several children together. Maita had the same opinion, but as the saying goes, love conquers all obstacles. When Neni saw that it was impossible to stop our romance, she even started giving us support. We went to parties together, to nightclubs, and any place that you can imagine. I was happy, she was happy, and that was all that mattered.

Of course I did not under any circumstances touch her, this we decided to do when we get married. I courted her for three solid months, then one beautiful Saturday night, I as usual asked her to go out with me, of course the twins were included, it was the first of June, 1955. We went to a restaurant, had dinner and then some drinks. The night was still young so we decided to buy some more drinks and go to a park, or even better, go to the outskirts of the city. My friend Yoshka was with us, he had a car, so it was easy to reach to the outskirts of the city. When we reached the place that looked inviting, we made ourselves as comfortable as possible on the grass under the stars, it was heaven on earth for me. I always carried my accordion with me, so we sang songs and said jokes up to the little hours of the night. Suddenly I realized that I could not let her go home again. I took her aside from the group, held her in my arms and kissed her like I never did before, and said, "Maita, let's elope." To my surprise she said she expected this for quite a while. Then I said, "Tonight." She did not say anything, but just moved her head up and down, I said, "We should tell our group of our plan," and she agreed. The twins only said that they will have a lot of trouble at home, but then Lola said for our happiness it was worthwhile, so they took us to a hotel by the name of Everest. The word elope does not mean escape, or kidnap, it just means we ran away together, with mutual understanding.

That's where it all started, the hotel was just around the corner from where I lived. The next morning I told her to wait for me in the hotel, so I could buy flowers and wine, and send to her through my youngest sister Zina. That was our custom, according to what my elders said. And then Zina could bring her home that very day. I reserved a big table in a nightclub where my musician friends played, and invited all my friends, and of course her parents and mine. She went with my sister to buy some clothes and all the things needed for the occasion, every thing was going according to plan. Our guests arrived, complimented us, we had our first dance officially married. There was no surprise, everybody knew it would happen sooner or later.

But something did happen that night, someone told my ex-wife that my wedding party was to be that night. 'Til today I don't know what got into her. Just as we were starting to have fun, she arrived with a Armenian friend of ours, a bad character, an opportunist and all the bad qualities you could find. They sat at a different table from ours, we saw them but we acted as if we did not. I went up the stage to play the accordion with my musician friends, when I noticed my ex-wife was drinking heavily, obviously to get drunk. I quickly went back to my table and told my guests that trouble was coming. I knew her very well, my ex-wife was unpredictable. Just as I finished talking to my friends she stood up and wanted to come to our table, but the Armenian took her by the arm and would not let her. Then she sat down for a minute, she was calm, suddenly she stood up again, but this time she took a bottle of whisky that was on the table, and smashed it on the table. The bottle broke, what was left in her hand was about half of the bottle, she then used it like a weapon on the Armenian. She aimed for the face, luckily he managed to step aside, but still she got him on one part of his face, and she wanted more, but the people near her table held her off. I did not wait to see the damage she had done to him, I grabbed Maita by the hand, and only had time to say to my guests that I was sorry that this happened. Someone said, "You go, we will be fine." That night we did not sleep at home. I was told later that night, she came with the police to claim me. In Iran in that period the police did not need a warrant to search your house. They just entered and did the job in my house, they even searched in the basement, and even under the beds. The next day my sister went to the police station and explained the situation and that was that, who suffered most about the situation was the Armenian.

On our honeymoon I took my wife Maita to Shemran, about thirty kilometers from Tehran. You travel all the way up so it's much cooler there. It's like a resort especially made for tourists.

During this time of the year it's Paradise, everything is blooming, the air is as sweet as honey, it is compared to the Swiss Alps. The village was dotted with small hotels very comfortable. There was only one big hotel with a nightclub, so during the night we sometimes went out to dance, those were the days I shall never forget 'til the end of my days. She was like a child, everything fascinated her, everything we did was fun, we did not think of tomorrow, simply we had no time for it, we shared everything what we had, and what we did not. 'Til today I never regretted my marriage, this kind of happiness very few people enjoy.

A month had passed and she was already pregnant, you can imagine how happy that made me. My ex-wife was seven years with me and could not give me a child, this is what I call destiny.

In Iran my work did not render much, mostly because my work was not regular. I depended a lot on private clubs, and also private parties, or even birthday parties. Let's say I was a freelance musician, but sometimes I made a contracts for a few months. That made me feel insecure, after all I was about to become a father, I needed something more solid. As I had a little experience in precious and semiprecious stones, I came up with an idea to put my experience to work, besides I had a few friendly Russian jewelers. I was very popular with my Russian music in the Russian colony. The town was small so almost everybody knew everybody else, because we all Christians stayed together and went to the same clubs and restaurants. So I had no trouble to find work with the jewelers, that is, during the day. At first I was hired as an appraiser of precious stones, then sometimes they needed stones like onyx, a semiprecious stone, and also garnets, which were very rare in Iran, so I had to go and buy for them in other countries. I was doing well now.

I was worried about my cousin, the father of my present wife, she was already three months pregnant, he was abroad and was about to return. If I was worried, imagine my wife and my sister Lida. I was told that he was already informed about our marriage, so we had to wait and see what happens. One morning I was going to work when I nearly bumped into him on the main street of the city. I looked up at him and smiled, I must have looked silly. I said, "You are back." "No," he said. "I am in Japan." That's actually where he came from. He was much taller than me and very good looking. I acted as if nothing has happened. Then he said, "Tell Lida that I am in Park Hotel, and to come as soon as possible," then he turned around and walked away. By the look of his face he was very angry, so I did not know what to expect of him. I went to a phone and told my employers that I would not be available this day. I even did not bother to give the reason. I practically ran all the way home. On the way I stopped to think. I could not by any means frighten my wife. I was afraid that she might lose the baby or get sick or something, so I had to somehow minimize the situation, even lie to her about my meeting with her father and say that every thing was normal between me and her father. When I arrived, I became as calm as possible, called my wife and my sisters to the living room, told them to sit down and told them that Tsino has arrived, that was her father's name. They were all quiet for a few seconds, then started to talk all in the same time. I quieted all of them down and said, "Please listen to me, all of you, the man was completely calm when I talked to him, he just asked me to tell his wife to come to him. He is accommodated in Park Hotel." We all knew that he has been informed about me and Maita, I know that he has known this for some time. We knew this through our twin cousins, they always informed us when their mother sent letters to her son. I estimated that two days after we eloped she informed him of the situation, so by now he must have took it for granted. The utmost he can do is try to avoid speaking to me and Maita, he also must be knowing about her pregnancy so there is nothing he can do about it. Maita started to cry and ran out of the room. My elder sister Olga ran after her. I wanted to follow, but the others would not let me. Someone said, "Let her cry a little, that will make her feel better." That night I had a hard time to persuade her that he must accept our marriage and that time will cure the bitterness he might have inside him. After all, my sister Lida is his wife, she will help him to forgive us. I am sure that we will laugh about this situation after a week or so. He came to our house, and Maita went to him and asked for his forgiveness, which he promptly accepted. As for me, it took quite a time before he spoke to me. He was a very proud man and very intelligent, he knew where to step back and where to go in front. Ever since I can remember I was his friend, in the early times we used to go out together, have fun, he liked the way I sang and played the accordion. When he started to court my sister, only I knew and a few more people. He knew that I know, but I pretended that I did not.

I must explain to my reader, that first-cousin marriages are taboo as far as our customs are concerned, that was the reason he did not stay with his mother, not that he did not want to, but because she would not have him. That is why my wife and her sister Lialia grew up seeing very little of him, although he provided all their needs. His mother never forgave him for marrying my sister. His mother was a very stubborn woman, and she proved it. She did not speak to him or to my sister for many years.

As I said, sometimes I had to travel for my work to buy stones. One day my boss told me to go to Baghdad, the capital of Iraq, and buy some stones from a man that I have already done business with him, for several times with great success. This time a lot of money were involved. I was anxious to close the deal as soon as possible. When I arrived in Baghdad I felt that there was a sort of unrest in the city, so I left as soon as I closed the deal.

When I arrived I decided that I will not leave to anywhere until Maita gives birth to our child. My father was on the verge of opening a nightclub, he was making a deal with a guy who owned a club and wanted to rent it, my father said it was a matter of time before he closed the deal. After a few days he told me to round up some musicians so that I could form a band. The club had about thirty tables and a big bar, it needed very little decoration to transform it into a nightclub. I was very excited about all this because I knew that the American colony, the Point Four, the NCO club, were all our customers. We did a little advertising but word got around quickly even before we opened the joint. I decorated my bandstand with neon lights which said "Vic's Band." I was very proud of it. For the first time in my life I was the leader of the band, and I had elder musicians under my command, and I simply loved what I was doing, although I did not earn a red cent. My father paid the musicians. The place was right in the heart of the city and it was called the Ramsar nightclub; we could not change the name for bureaucratic reasons. The nightclub was an immediate success. My father was very happy. It's been a long time since he operated a nightclub and made money of his own. He was proud of himself and we, his children, knew it, and were all there to help him. My sisters were all behind the bar serving drinks with other nice looking girls, mostly Russian or Assyrian, who spoke English and Russian, and also Iranian. We needed to hire a good manager to organize things. My father could not do it alone. There were too much things to be done. We also served food, international food to be exact, we also had Iranian customers mostly from the high societies. At that time only our nightclub had girls behind the bar, this was something new in Tehran. We were expecting some trouble from the government for putting girls behind the bar but it did not come. Amazingly, the trouble came from a different direction.

The husbands of my sisters, every single night they used to come and watch their wives work, this went on for quite a while. Only my sister Zina was free from the jealousy of her boy friend, because she was a good crooner and worked with me most of the time. My father made a lot of money, but one day he was forced to dismiss my sisters to save their marriages, so he had to hire some other girls to take the places of my sisters. But to find girls who spoke English was not easy, and even when you found one, they asked for fifty percent for every drink they drank with the customer. Of course the drink was almost all Coca-Cola, just a few drops of vodka was included to give it a smell of alcohol. Of course there were exceptions, some girls liked to drink occasionally, they insisted that the drink be legitimate. There were other drinks like champagne, wine, whisky etc., etc., but vodka Coke was the favorite at that time in Iran The local drink by the name of *kishmish* was used mostly by the lower-class people. We were very careful that our girls would not exaggerate on their drinks. After all this is a Muslim country, to see a drunk woman in the club or on the streets was almost impossible. We did not admit to have a bad name of our nightclub. If the girl wanted to go out with somebody she had to go out when she finished her job with us, what she did outside the nightclub was her business, we had no responsibility whatsoever. So we became famous overnight. Before long other nightclubs followed our example, but there was room for everybody. What the other clubs did not have was experience. We had it from China, particularly with American and foreign personnel. We held on to the nightclub for over a year.

My son Latsi was born, I remember the night she had the pains, I was terrified. My sisters took her to the hospital, luckily the hospital was only a few blocks away. Latsi was born on the 9th of April, 1956. I bought a box of cigars, invited all my friends to come to the hospital, and bought a lot of flowers. Before entering the hospital we all went and had a few drinks to give me courage to face Maita. After what she went through I thought she would, blame me for her pains, but that was all my imagination. When she saw me and my friends she was very happy to see us, and at the same time she felt ashamed. We were so many that the nurse said for everybody to leave except the father of the child, so I stayed. I could not find the right words to tell her of my feelings, I never experienced such emotion before. All I said was, "Did you see our son?" She said, "Yes," and that they will bring him shortly, for her to feed the child. Then my sister Olga entered and told me to go and get rid of my friends, because they were disturbing the peace of the hospital. I did just that, but not before I said, "I will be back to see my son."

We lost the nightclub because the owner refused to renew our contract. He saw the success we had and he wanted a part of it, but the conditions he gave us were absurd, so we gave him back his club. He started to work without us, after a few months he shut down the club for lack of experience.

So again I started to do my old job, but this time I had to travel more frequently, I was asked to go and buy a few hundred carats of turquoise, a semiprecious stone very popular in the Middle Eastern countries, especially in Iran. I had to travel to Baghdad for them. My son was already more than a year old, and my wife was already pregnant for several months. I decided to take my wife with me. This was a big mistake. When we arrived in Baghdad we went to a hotel where most foreigners of middle class go to, it was a little expensive, but I wanted my wife to be more comfortable. There were a lot of foreign reporters and we made some friends in the lobby and talked about all sorts of things, including politics. One of them by the name of George, I don't remember his surname. We were two to three nights in the hotel, when this reporter George told me about the situation in the country. He said something was brewing very serious in the country that it made us feel it might explode any minute. I did not pay to much attention to his remarks, anyway it made me feel uneasy, my wife was not present when he told me that.

I usually did not take so much time to close the deal, but the man who sold me the stones was not in Baghdad, so I had to wait for his return. In the meantime I showed my wife the city, visiting historic places like ordinary tourists having a good time. Little did we know what will happen to us on the next day.

As usual we woke up early in the morning. We were getting ready to take a bath, when there was a knock on the door. It was George. He looked very nervous and said, "There is a coup rumored," saying the King Faysal II has been killed last night, and that there are guards at the door of the hotel, preventing anybody to leave or enter the hotel, all the radio stations were announcing a republican government, headed by some military officer called Abdul-Karim Qassim.

I must explain that this was the time the first Russian rocket went into space and a first device was circling the world by the name of Sputnik. That made us feel bad. My wife worried that there may be some shooting going on the streets. Later on we actually heard some gunfire but it was far from the hotel. I tried to calm my wife, but to no avail, as if she sensed that something bad will happen to us. I asked George why they would not let at least the reporters out of the hotel to cover the story, but he said that the officer in charge had orders not to let anybody out or in and will not say why. Our hotel was on the main street. The management told us to clear out from the windows, that stray bullets might enter, and they were right. We stayed from the windows as far as possible. Practically the whole staff of the hotel were listening to the radio, every now and then a waiter a friend of mine would come and tell me the latest news, he spoke very well in English, and George was there with me, noting all that he said and gave a tip every time the news was of interest to him. We heard crowds shouting on the streets. I remember that the waiter said that the king was shot, with two English girls in his bed, at five in the morning.

I must explain to the reader, that who was running the country not King Faysal, but his uncle. He was about to be nominated, but he did not make it. His father died when he was a child, so his uncle took over as his tutor until he becomes of age to be crowned. He was the first cousin of the present King of Jordan, Hussein. I don't know his exact age, he must have been not more than nineteen years old.

Then the waiter came again and said that his uncle was also was shot, then tied by the legs to a truck, and hurled through the streets while the crowds cheered. Late that night George and I were informed by the same source that the Prime Minister was caught on the train in Basra, Iraq, trying to cross the border to Iran. He was said to be dressed like a woman and used a veil to cover his face like the Arab tradition demands. Some say that his aides betrayed him. And he was also instantly killed right on the train station. He was literally torn apart by the crowd, the country hated him, he was considered a British spy.

Two days passed before they came to inspect us, they got hold of our passports and started interrogating us one by one. When my turn came I was a little nervous, they asked me if I could speak in Arabic. I said no, so they asked for an interpreter. I was the only Iranian in the hotel, and my family of course. When the man came he was more nervous than I was. I had nothing to hide, as for the stones, I always paid five percent on the border to the government, of the total amount of the stones, and I had previous transaction papers to prove it, I always carried the papers with me to be on the safe side. The first thing they asked me was what was my business here. I told them that I came to buy stones. There were three officers in the room and the interpreter. One said, "You lie." I was astonished by his remark. Then they asked who was my friend in the hotel. I had no friend in the hotel, just acquaintances, again he said, "You lie, we know that you and George are working together, you were always informed by the waiter what was happening in the country, you and your wife are under arrest until further notice, go to your room and stay there and send your wife to us." There is no words to describe my misery. What will happen to us now? My first thought was to inform my embassy, but what will I tell my wife? I was completely confused, I did not know my right from my left.

I was escorted by a soldier to my room. When I came to the door of my room the soldier told me to stop, then he put his hand in his pocket came out with a bunch of keys, selected the key of my room number and opened the door. That means my wife was locked in, that made me feel even worse than I already was. When I came into the room my wife was sitting in the arm chair with my son on her lap, she quickly put my son aside and ran to me and hugged me with all her might, she was crying and said with a trembling voice, "What is happening? Please tell me." My son, seeing his mother cry, he also began to cry. I was desperate. I tried to calm her down, but she could not stop sobbing, it took about five minutes before she came to. I told her to calm the boy, because I had very important things to tell her. I said that it was between life and death. "They asked me to tell you to go down and answer some questions, please tell them the truth. They said we are under arrest, so this may be the last time we will be together until they find out that we had nothing to do with the situation". The soldier opened the door and told me to hurry. I told her to give me a little money, she took all the money out and wanted to give to me all, but I said no. I just took about twenty percent of the amount, and I said, "You will need it on your way back to Iran." She started to cry again, then I said, "Please be strong, now you have a big responsibility on your hands, your son and the one that on its way, you may be locked up two to three days, but with me it's a different story, because they think I am involved with George in politics. If they ask you about George, say that we met him here and never saw him before in our lives." Again the soldier interrupted. I had to give him a note to keep quiet for a few minutes. I said to her to demand the presence of our Iranian consul, but deep inside I knew that now this country considered Iranians as enemies, for the simple reason that we had a king, and they just killed theirs. I stayed behind, and the soldier took my wife and son away. That was the last time I saw my wife in Iraq.

I waited in our room for her to come back, a million thoughts passed through my head. At that time I used to smoke. I smoked a cigarette after another every two to three minutes. I looked at my watch. I even tried to open the door but it was locked, but then after what seemed to be a lifetime I heard the key turn in the lock, and the door opened. An officer was standing there. He did not bother to come in, but waved his hand to come with him. I followed him through the corridor. He opened another door and called me. The room was empty. He walked out of the door, locked it behind him, and I was left alone again. Now it was obvious they did not want me to see my wife until they come to a decision. Our clothes were all in the other room. Another hour passed, again they took me to our room, only this time the room was empty, but my suitcase was on the bed waiting there for me to pick it up. So my wife was here and packed my things, her suitcase was not in sight. I asked him where was my wife but he would not answer, just pointed to my suitcase to take it out. I did so and followed him out of the room. Something happened to me that I shall never forget, some sort of force got hold of me, the fear suddenly left me and I seemed immune to everything come what may. I thought, "I put myself and my family in God's hands." I remember it started to rain. My thoughts were with my wife and child. I was bitter but at the same time angry.

They took me to a jeep. I got in. There were two officers in the jeep waiting for me. I wanted to say something, but the officer put his finger to his lips to keep me silent. We traveled for about twenty minutes before we arrived to a big red building. When we stopped for the first time they handcuffed me and took me on the first floor to an office where a high-ranking officer was at a desk waiting for us. The building was like a bee hive, there were soldiers, officers, running up and down like madmen with papers in their hands, and even bumping into each other in the corridors. The high-ranking officer told them to take off my handcuffs, and told me to sit down, and ordered the men who brought me to leave, but not before he signed a paper that the officer who brought me gave him. I was left alone with him in the room. To my surprise he did not even look at me, he took some other papers and started to study them. I was wondering what officially will we be charged with, to charge me as a spy was absurd, they had no evidence whatsoever. Just because I talked to a reporter, was that a crime? Then I thought, "Maybe during such times of revolution what they are doing is part of their security." I thought, "Within a few days they will deport us to Iran."

I stayed in that room with the officer at least for five hours. Every now and then they would bring a foreigner to him. He looked at the papers of the man, then sent him off somewhere, when finally he looked at me and said, "You will be taken to another place which deals only on Iranian affairs, you must wait when they come for you, I don't know the time, we are all very tired. Besides, you have nowhere to hurry. All this will take time, only Allah knows how long it will take, he said that more out of tiredness than to explain the situation. It was in the early hours in the morning when they came to take me away, this time I was handcuffed again and taken to a prison truck. When they pushed me in it was so dark I could not see an inch from my nose, but I felt there were a lot of people with me, the stench was horrible. It was so full that I felt like a sardine in a can, but I did not mind, all I thought, if they treated my wife the same way as they do with me. But then I thought, my little son was with her, they would not dare treat her this way, or would they? After all we are not in a jungle, we are in Baghdad, the capital of Iraq, a more or less a civilized country. Only God knows what came to my head, at that black hour I prayed quietly, just as I had begun to have a wonderful life, this had to happen. I cursed myself a million times because I brought my wife and child with me, but then, she wanted to come, so much it was like a second honeymoon, I just could not refuse her.

We arrived at a big building what looked like a big prison. We were put in line and marched into the prison, now I could look around me and see who my co-prisoners were. To my surprise they were all mostly Kurds. I could say by their dress, only a few were dressed like me. I heard that the Kurdish provinces in Iraq were fighting for their independence for decades, and they were all commies supported by Russia, then I understood that I was taken to a political prison. What made me feel cold in my stomach, was that they were torturing political prisoners at will. Somebody told me that, I think it was George, if I am not mistaken, but then I was not a Kurd nor a commie. After all, I am an ex-refugee from a communist country, but how can I prove it? They lined us up again and called each of us by name, we were about twenty to twenty-five prisoners. They divided us and took us to a cell. I was accompanied by four Kurds, all young men, none was over twenty-five years old. In the cell there was nothing, only the floor was covered with papers, old newspapers, to be exact. There was a single electric bulb which was too bright for my comfort. Before entering the cell we were relieved of everything we had on us, including our belts and even our shoe laces. We were not allowed to talk to each other. The door of the cell was cage-like, a soldier was always there to see if we had any conversations, every hour or so one of us was taken out for interrogation, but he never returned. Within a few hours I was left alone, then they brought new prisoners, the same thing happened to them, throughout the night this was happening. To go to the toilet was almost impossible. It depended upon the mood of the guard. I was wondering why I was not called. Maybe, I thought, they want to contact my embassy. Later they told me that even my embassy was surrounded by their troops, that meant the personnel of the embassy were virtually prisoners. The country was in a mess, they awaited some kind of an uprising from its own people or the neighboring countries like Iran or Jordan, and with reason, because both countries were kingdoms.

Finally my turn came to be interrogated. I was taken again by jeep to some building nearby the prison. They took me to a room. It was empty except for a table and four chairs. They told me to sit on one of the chairs and went away, but not before locking the door behind them. I waited for about an hour or so, when suddenly the door opened and two officers came in. I stood up as a respect to them, but I don't think they understood my move. One of them told me to sit down. He spoke in Iranian very well. They were in possession of my documents. They looked over it then asked my full name, and all other formalities, then one said suddenly, how long was I working for George? I said I never worked for George or anyone else, then with out warning he gave me a slap on the face that nearly threw me of the chair, and said, "This is just a sample, if you lie again we will take more drastic measures, you are a spy and can be shot if you don't cooperate." Then I said, "Please bring my consul, he must have all my records, if you don't believe me, you have to believe my consul." They both started to laugh, then one said, "He is as much a spy as you are." Before they wanted to ask some more questions, luck came my way, suddenly the door burst open and a very high official came in. They stood up at attention for him. He came to the table, took up the papers, looked over them for about five minutes or so, then looked up and started to laugh. He said something to them in a loud voice, then showed them something on my papers and laughed again, looked at me and walked away. When he left the officers started to argue among themselves for quite a while, then what seemed to me that they came to an agreement. The officer that talked in Iranian said, "You are lucky. You were just taken away from our responsibility, you are to go to a political prison and await your trial." They stood up and went away, visibly upset.

I was taken to another prison. I was surprised to see at the difference. The cells were clean and there were beds with mattresses, sheets, and even pillows, the prisoners were clean and every cell held about ten prisoners, the doors of the cells were open up 'til six in the afternoon, we could walk in the compound at will. And the most important thing was that we could talk to anyone whenever we wish to. The food was good, I mean for a prison, but later I found out that for the common criminal the food was terrible. We also could send letters home. This was what kept me alive.

I made a lots of friends, especially Christian Arabs. For us Christians was a separate cell, but I made myself a rule never to talk about politics. What made me popular among my co-prisoners that I spoke English and other languages. I received my first letter from home after two months of my detention, my wife wrote that she also was detained for forty days before she was deported to Iran, and that she was fine and was living with my father. The letter picked up my morale to such an extent that I hardly slept that night. There were also some money in the envelope for me to buy cigarettes. I wrote her that I was forgotten in the prison, several times I asked my friends to write an appeal to the local justice authorities to take me to trial or to come to some kind of decision. Almost three months passed since my arrest, but there was no reply.

To give an idea to the reader what was like to live in an Arabian political prison is that it was not easy, especially for us Christians, there were always conflicts between us, for instance, when they pray we have to go to our cells and hardly make a noise, so that they may not feel that we are mocking their religion. When the food arrived we were not allowed to go first to take it, we were always the last. Even when we washed our dishes or clothes, they had their time, we had ours, we practically did not mix with them, although they were commies, there was a lot of drugs and homosexual activities. We Christians had a sort of different diversion, like chess games, football, volleyball, etc., etc, but nevertheless we had our black sheep. One of my friends by the name of Timor, I caught him red-handed having sex with a Muslim youngster. It was a hot afternoon and all of us during this period of time were out of our cells walking in the compound, then I remembered that I had something to write. I was going to my cell to do it. When I entered and saw that they were having sex, I quickly turned around and went away, but he saw me after this he would not talk to me, and if he did only in front of the others, but only to provoke me, he wanted me out of the cell, he was afraid that I would tell everyone about his shameful act as a Christian. For the Arabs this type of sex was normal, when a new prisoner arrived very young and nice looking, the leaders of each cell made deals between them who would be the first to have sex with the youngster, sometimes money was involved, some times even fights. I have seen that many of them went to hospitals gravely hurt. So one night just after they close the cells, Timor wanted to have a fight with me, and in front of every one he asked me if I knew how to fight, I asked him why. He said he wanted to test my strength with him. I said I had no reason to do so, but he insisted he was much taller than me and a few years younger, so I thought I will have to face him. I did not want to leave the cell under any circumstances, because I had other good friends who helped me in many ways, like writing appeals to the authorities, and besides I did not want to lose my face in front of the others. I had one advantage against him that he did not know, it was the street fights which I learned in China, and had to use against drunk sailors, and other hooligans, who sometimes invaded our bars. I only wondered if I was still good at it. Within seconds he was on the ground screaming as a woman, in pain with both of his hands holding testicles. I wanted to kick him in the face but my other friends stopped me. I used only one kick to finish him off, the street fight paid off. After that I had his respect, not only his but also the rest of the compound, word got around quickly. Even the guards knew about it, because fights amongst Christians was rare, if not impossible. After a day or so I was called to see the warden, he asked me about the fight. I said we were just training, and he said, "Because you lie, I sentence you to three days in solitary." The cell was very small, completely empty, the door was made of wood. When they pushed me in and closed the door I was in complete darkness. When I found the wall I let myself slide down to the ground. When I sat I felt that the ground was of mud and wet. Every morning they opened the door so I may go to the toilet, then they would throw a few buckets of water on the ground of my cell on purpose, so that I would not lie down. To eat they would give me a piece of bread and a can of water, 'til about six in the afternoon, then they would come again and do it all over again. When I came back to our compound I was cheered by my friends, and even Timor, because I did not reveal the true story, because if I did, Timor would have been sentenced as well.

So now that I received letters and also replied, life seemed to have a meaning. A funny thing happened to me at the prison. One morning I heard my name being called. I ran to the main door like a madman. The officer on the other side of the door had some papers in his hands, then he shouted some other names. I knew this officer by sight. He was the one who usually took prisoners to court. I just could not believe that at last I was wanted by the court. I asked him again if I was wanted. He said, "Is your name Victor?" I said, "Yes." He opened the main door and asked me to come out. I was dazed with happiness. Others also came out. There were four soldiers besides the officer and they took us to a bus, but before doing that they handcuffed us, but I did not mind. I was so happy, I thought freedom is near at last. I knew I was innocent of any accusations. We arrived at the justice building. We did not enter the main door, but they took us around the building. There was a small door which took us to a big hall, which was separated by cage-like cells. We were told to enter in to one of those cells and wait to be called. When finally the officer came and took me out of the cell I was very nervous, I hardly could control myself. I remember we went upstairs and entered a hall with a lot of people sitting in theater-like chairs, then I saw the judge. When I got closer, I saw that there was also a jury. There was a stand for only one man to stand and the officer took me to it. I was facing the judge about five feet from me, of course he was sitting behind a big desk a few feet higher than all of us, and dressed in a black robe. Then a man came to me and announced that he was the interpreter. Before long the prosecutor came to my interpreter and said something I did not understand. The interpreter asked me where was I, let's say, a month ago, and he said the date. I was surprised, but I promptly answered, "In jail." He said, "What?" I said again, "In prison." He told this to the prosecutor, "Is his name Victor?" I said, "Yes," but Victor what? Then he started to look in the papers in his hand. He seemed confused, and went to look for other papers. The interpreter told me very softly, "You did not kill your wife?" I said, "You must be crazy. My wife is in Iran." The prosecutor went to the judge said something to him. The judge instantly dismissed me.

This is to give the reader an idea how Iraqi justice worked, all the system of the government have changed, in their place the army rebels took over with no experience whatsoever. I was given work to take care of the administration offices. I had other four prisoners under my command to keep clean the area. To get there I had to cross the entire prison. I saw ex-generals, ex-governors, judges, and high officials crammed in one cell and begging for food or cigarettes. They were treated beyond human comprehension. I personally felt sorry for them, but there was nothing that I could do. Occasionally I would throw them some bread and cigarettes when nobody was around to see what I did, otherwise I would have been in trouble myself. Every time I passed I could see that they were tortured, and some were taken away never to be seen again, I saw that because the cell that they were in was cage-like. The soldiers would pass and spit on them, or poke their sticks in their bodies, the ones who were near the door. There were thirty to forty of them in the beginning, but when I finally left there were only three left.

But let me tell the reader how I was allowed to leave. Amazingly the Iranian government did not break relationship with Iraq, so my wife went with a lawyer to the Embassy of Iraq and were trying to get me out through diplomatic sources, this took time and money. Finally I was informed that I was to be deported. I could hardly wait, then one morning they came after me and took me to a police station, there they put me in a cell with six other Iranian citizens. They told me openly that they were common criminals, by now nothing surprised me. We were all to wait 'til sundown, before they take us to the railway station. Our destination was Basra, Iraq. I was too excited to eat, to drink, I just wanted to be on my way to home. I was already six months and some days in prison. I did not know I had such an ability to survive. When I came home I had a beautiful daughter that I have never seen. Her name is Zina. I named her after my youngest sister.

To a Gypsy freedom is everything in life, we are said to be born free. We are scattered all around the globe, the reason is only one, to seek freedom. And today the world has finally came to its senses, its almost free. Only a few are still under the communist rule, but the day will come, when there will be no frontiers between countries, that will truly be freedom.

73

My return was marked by a lot of sadness, my mother died while I was still in prison. They did not write me about it, not to give me more sufferings than I already had. My father just could not live without my mother, he was constantly sick and visibly lost interest in life. He could have lived more, but my mother's death had a terrific impact upon his health, and the doctor said he had very little time left to live. I wanted not to believe the doctor, but he was right. He died shortly after my mother's death.

Without my parents there was nothing to hold me in Iran. I made a reunion with my sisters and told them that I had plans to go to Brazil. Because we had some relatives there, and the country was full of opportunity, and that it was a free country for all races without discrimination, and was receiving immigrants from all countries, and it was very easy to receive permanent visas. I wanted to immigrate to the States but I had to wait for at least five years.

Earlier in this book I promised my reader that I shall write about my sister's daughter, who married the Anglo-Indian. She had already three children from her husband. As a British subject he was constantly harassed by the local Iranian police to leave the country, so they had to leave to England. His all family was already there. She left one of her sons, Douglas, to be exact, for my sister to care. Because she was the only daughter she did not want to leave her mother and father without somebody to care for. So just about the very same time we were deciding what our destination will be, to leave Iran for good, a letter came from England. It was from the sister of Robin, the husband of my sister's daughter, stating that her daughter Zina had been murdered by her husband. It was a terrific blow to all of us, it was in the newspaper called the Daily Mirror, in London, and later the story was front page in Tehran, stating that an Englishman murdered an Iranian woman. Reporters came to my sister's house for more details. For a week or so my sister was hospitalized. Later I went to the British Embassy to ask for the newspaper. They promptly gave it to me. The reason of the murder was, according

Zina and Robin Davidson. (National Archives UK: PRO.)

to the paper, jealousy, he was jealous of his own brother, it also said that he poisoned her, and that he confessed.

This situation made us even more determined to leave Iran. If the local police would have let her husband stay in Iran this tragedy could not have happened. We decided to go to the Brazilian consulate to apply for entry visa, but to our surprise he said we had to wait for at least two years. We were all sad about it, but our relatives in Brazil said it was easy to take a visa, so we wrote to them about the situation. The answer we got was astonishing. It seems that in Calcutta, India, they somehow made friends with the consul of Brazil and he also baptized one of their children, so he became a godfather to the family, and that way he somehow arranged an entry visa for them. They advised us to go to Calcutta and meet him, and that they will send a letter to him to help us get the visa as soon as possible. But this was a shot in the dark. I had to sell my father's properties, a few houses that he bought and rented. I also sold my apartment, and all what was in it. My sister Olga did likewise, my other sisters were left behind. They said if our trip to India was a success then they would follow us and meet us in Brazil.

So again we took the same route back, but before leaving we sent a letter to the consul. He was on leave and would be back within a month's time, so we had all the time in the world. We arrived in Bombay just in about ten days, we were lucky to catch the ship in Khorramshahr, otherwise we would have to wait for a couple of weeks in Khorramshahr and spend a lot of money in vain. Then we had to cross the whole peninsula of India to get to Calcutta by train. Of course I personally liked the trip, because it was very punctual. The only thing I did not like was that there was no restaurant aboard, you had to order your food in one station and get it in the other.

When we arrived we went to the same hotel, and we were welcomed by the same owner of the hotel, what made us happy that some our relatives were also there. So it was like old times. They gave us a party as tradition asks, and two days later after the hangover was gone we returned the party, as tradition asks. We very much wanted them to accompany us to the consulate, but they had no passports, they were stateless. They told us that they had applied for Indian citizenship, and that it will take a lot of time before they will receive it, but they promised that once they get it they would follow us to Brazil. We still were not sure if we will receive the visa, then the bad news came the consul was transferred to the Philippines, so we had no choice but to follow him. We came so far so we could not return under any circumstances. From Calcutta there was a ship every month or so that made the trip to Japan, via Rangoon, Burma, Singapore now Malaysia, then came Hong Kong, There we had to change ships to arrive in Manila, the capital of the Philippines.

Surprisingly there were still some Gypsy refugees in Hong Kong, waiting to be shipped out as immigrants to such countries as Argentine, Bolivia, and even Brazil. Of course we knew each other way back from China, they were not our relatives but we grew up together, that was more than enough for a celebration. The ship we traveled on was of the same company of the ships that took us to Iran, but only larger. The food, as I have mentioned before, was horrible, so we asked the purser to change our food from European to Chinese food, because the crew was Chinese, so this time we even enjoyed the trip. When we arrived in Hong Kong we took a hotel, so immediately I went to the local immigration office and asked where the Gypsies lived in Hong Kong, because a lot of them were already immigrated to other countries. He told me yes, they were held in a refugee camp, sustained by the famous American organization of IRO. We had to have a special permission to see them, we celebrated the event in the camp. Their movements were controlled by the local police, each person had to return to camp before midnight, but any way we had a lot of fun while it lasted.

Our trip to Manila by ship was a bumpy one, because we had a little storm, it was a forty-eight hour trip, but our women did not eat practically nothing, due to seasickness. In Manila we finely met the consul. He was very polite to us, and said that he will do his best to give us the visa, but he asked for time, at least a week or so. That made us feel very happy, a week was not to much to wait. Again our fate was in the hands of somebody else, but we had faith in God, up 'til now He never let us down.

By now my wife was pregnant for the third time. We Gypsies love to have a lot of children, yet now I sometimes think whether our race will survive, we are mixing too much with other races, that makes me feel bad. The ignorant Gipsies don't mix so much as we do, because we go to schools, and usually have higher standards of living. The pure-blooded Gypsies are becoming rare, I am proud to be one of them.

The consul made good his word, and promptly issued our visas. They were not ordinary visas but entry visas (that's the reason we wanted this type of visa to Brazil). When we arrive in Brazil we had a right to apply for permanent visas, and that picked up our morale, and we were getting ready to make the big leap from Asia to the Americas.

There was no direct ship from the Philippines to Brazil, to fly it never occurred to me, because I was afraid. I never flew in my life, so it was out of the question. There was an American line going to the States, via Hong Kong, Japan, Honolulu, and San Francisco, the ship's name was President Cleveland. It was a big liner, about sixty thousand tons, but we needed an American transit visa to change ships in the States. We were told that there was a Japanese liner that went from Los Angeles to Rio de Janeiro Brazil. So now we needed only the American transit visa to get to our destination. We went to the US consulate. The consul, amazingly, was a woman, she received us politely and we promptly gave her our passports to inspect. She saw our entry visas to Brazil and said, "Gentlemen, why don't you fly to Brazil?" I said that I was terrified to fly, she smiled and said, "Alright, then I will give you a transit visa good for only thirty days." I did not believe my ears. Now she said, "You have to make an oath, pick up your right hands please." We did as she said. "Do you promise under oath that you shall not try to stay in the US, or try to work while you are there?" "We do." "Leave your passports here and come tomorrow, they will be ready by then."

I wanted to kiss her, but I controlled myself, she just made my dream come true. I always wanted to see the US, and at last I will. When we got on the street, I was jumping in the air like a kid. I saw with my own eyes how the Americans helped us in China, not only us but whole world, thousands upon thousands of refugees were cared for through the organization of IRO and given a new chance to start life again, but people have short memories. I always up 'til today stand for the American people and always will, for me the really free country is the USA.

Our ship was leaving on the thirty-first of December on the eve of the New Year of 1959, our destination, San Francisco. The ship had only two classes, saloon class and tourist class. We took tourist class, naturally we had to economize, we had a long way to go. We had to buy tickets for the Japanese liner to Brazil, and we did not know what the price of the tickets were, but the tourist class was not bad, we had good cabins, the food was excellent, there were two different kinds of food served at once, one was American, the other was Chinese. We even had a big hall with a bar where we could have a drink, and even dance, during Saturdays with live music. The musicians came from the saloon class to play for us during the day of course.

The ship had to dock in Hong Kong to pick up passengers, so we had another chance to see our people. I left the ship alone, because my wife was over six months pregnant and did not feel so good, and my brother-in-law did not want to go either. When I arrived at their camp, I was surprised to see that our people were not there. It seems they did not want to stay in the camp anymore, so the IRO moved them to a hotel where only foreign refugees were allowed to stay. I asked the address and promptly found them again. There was a lot fun, but they wanted to see the rest of the family. We had to go to the shipping company to get special passes for them to get aboard. Only three people were allowed, the rest were very sad about it. I was told the ship will leave within twenty-four hours, so we had very little time. I took them aboard and they saw the rest of the family, then we went to the bar and started to drink, aboard the drinks were very cheap, so we drank a little more than necessary. Time was short ,so we had to leave the ship, but I was a little high, so I insisted to take them to the hotel. We had about four hours left, so I thought I had a lot of time. My wife tried to stop me but to no avail, so we left the ship. On the way we stopped to have another drink. While having the drink in a small bar, two Chinese men came in, there was nobody there but us and the two men that came in, except the barman. To our surprise one of the men took a gun out of his pocket and announced a stickup. They took everything we had, including my gold watch, Omega, a few hundred dollars, then they walked away peacefully. That sobered me up instantly. Now I had no money for the taxi. Somehow the barman borrowed some money from a friend and gave it to me. When I arrived on the dock, they were getting ready to raise the gangway, I arrived just in time. Lucky me, otherwise I would have been left behind, and my family would have gone to the States without me. This shows a few drinks more or less can change a lot of things in life, but thank God we left for Japan in peace.

In Yokohama a lot of Russian families boarded the ship, also refugees on their way to the US. One of the families was half-Gypsy, we knew their parents from Shanghai, so we were not alone on this long trip, we had someone to talk to, and also share ideas for the future. In all it took twenty-two days to reach our destination. While crossing the Pacific, for thirteen days we did not see land, just the sky and the sea. Luckily we had good weather.

When we arrived in Honolulu we passed the famous Pearl Harbor memorial, it stands in the middle of the harbor, that's where the ships were sunk during the Second World War. There were a lot of tourists visiting the memorial. I thought to myself, even on such terrible places somebody was making a lot of money from the tourists, thousands of young sailors lost their lives on those ships, and now everything was gone and forgotten, time has washed away all the bitterness of the Second World War, but not to everyone. The families of those young sailors will never forget their misfortune, this is a cruel world, but let us not get sad.

We went ashore to see a bit of Honolulu, we took a lot of photos, there were a lot of sailors on the streets, it reminded me of Shanghai after the war. What I noticed also was, when we aimed our cameras at the local young women, they usually covered their faces with their hands, they did not want to be photographed by any means. I thought this must be some sort of superstition.

We were also surprised to see many Gypsy young girls telling fortune on the main street. One came up to me and said in English, give your left hand, put a dollar in it, and I will tell you your fortune, they usually ask for the left hand because it is nearer to the heart. Then I said in Gypsy, "You also tell fortune to Gypsies?" She immediately blushed and let my hand go. She turned from me and ran to the others and said in a loud voice, "These two are Gypsies." By their dress and by their speech I knew they were from the Kelderasa tribe, the one that I described earlier in my book. I asked if they could take us to their elders. It was not too far away from where we were. Someone went ahead. When we arrived the elders were waiting for us. We were greeted warmly and were invited in, soon there was food and drinks on the table, we promptly said that we had a ship to catch, and that we had a very short time left. I did not want to make the mistake again like I did in Hong Kong. Anyway, they asked us from what tribe we were from. We said that we were Lovara. This word Lovara always brought surprised looks, particularly when we said that we were Russian Lovara. (I call myself a Russian Gypsy because my father was raised there, and he considered himself a Russian Gypsy.) It seems that in Russia our tribe was feared for some reason or another. One thing is sure, my people are taller in size, and European-like, we're more civilized, our men. I will not say that we are a superior race among Gypsies, but this particular tribe was always conservative and would not change with time. They insisted that we at least have a glass of beer, we did so not to offend them. Then I asked, were there many Gypsies in Honolulu. They said no, only a few families, they were from the mainland, to be exact from California, they lived in San Francisco and were here on a vacation, and that they live in America for at least half a generation, and were also immigrants from Russia, and that they heard about our tribe, they also said that we were the first Lovara they have ever seen. This time we did as we said and left very quickly, but before leaving they gave their addresses for us to visit them in San Francisco.

One thing is good among all Gypsies through out the world, a Gypsy in distress will always be helped by other Gypsies, but first he must prove that he or she is a Gypsy, you must speak Gypsy, and you must explain your origin, no false Gypsy is attended under any circumstances. No matter what your tribe, you are accepted as equal, this is a rule, but there are exceptions of course, The rich do not follow this rule so much as the middle class do. One thing is certain, we stick together when we have trouble with strangers. They took us to the ship to say farewell to the rest of the family.

Finally our last stop was San Francisco, USA. We were supposed to arrive early in the morning on the fourth day from Honolulu, but on the second day at sea the ship started to roll. Funny, there was no storm, but just very windy, and the wind blew harder every hour that passed. I personally don't get seasickness, but this time I felt a bit dizzy. My wife and my sister could not even get out of the cabin. The nearer we got to San Francisco the harder the ship rolled. Food was out of the question for my family, when I came to the dining room it was almost empty, only a few people had lunch or dinner. When the waiters brought the food they hardly could put it in the table, but when they did manage, I had to hold the plate in one hand and the fork in the other. To get the food to your mouth you had to be fast as a magician, otherwise you would spill your food on the table, no it was not easy. Nobody was allowed on the deck. Later that night it calmed down somewhat, the officer told me that at five in the morning we shall see the famous Golden Gate bridge if the ship did not roll to much. I asked him if this rolling of the ship is customary. As a matter of fact it is. He said that almost every time we are nearing San Francisco the sea gets rough a bit. To him it was just a bit, but to my family it was just a matter of time before the ship will sink. Nevertheless I and my brother-in-law woke up at four in the morning to see the Golden Gate bridge. It was, or still is, a magnificent view. It was still dark at this hour, the lights on the bridge made it look like a giant woman's diamond necklace. To my surprise a lot of people was on the deck to see the bridge.

We docked safely. After what we passed through it was a relief to be ashore. We went to a hotel on Market Street, it was a middle-class hotel but very comfortable. The first thing my brother-in-law did was to telephone to his cousin who lived in Las Vegas, she could hardly believe that we were in the States. Immediately she invited us to see her. She could not come because she worked in one those big casinos dealing cards, like baccarat or twenty-one, etc., etc. We had not seen her since 1946. We told her that first we must confirm our tickets for Brazil, and than we could come to see her if time permitted. When we went to buy our tickets, we were informed we could only buy them from Los Angeles because the ship that went to Brazil stopped only there, so we had to go there. Los Angeles is a very big city, the hotels are very expensive. We had to look for a apartment which could be hired for at least a couple of weeks or a month, because we were told that the ship we needed passed through Los Angeles every forty days or so. When we finally bought the tickets, they told us that the ship will arrive in about thirty days, so we had a lot of time to visit the cousin of my brother-in-law. I remember we hired a car to go to Las Vegas. I had an international driver's license, so we had no trouble hiring a car. It was a brand new 1960 Chevy. We had a hard time finding the route to Las Vegas but eventually we did, but not before driving around for a couple hours.

We arrived in Las Vegas. It was about midnight, but the town had just begun to live, there was a lot of traffic, and the neon lights lit up the whole town like a Christmas tree, the signs in neon lights advertised the names of big stars, like Dean Martin, or Sammy Davis, Junior, etc., etc. I was completely stunned by the night life of the city. Oh, yes, I heard about it, but to see it was something completely different. I wanted with all my soul to be part of it, to go from one casino to the other, to see all the shows if possible, but there was a catch to it now. I was a father of two, and one more was on its way, then I told myself, I will ask permission from my wife to go and see the night life for at least a couple of hours. I knew she will not refuse me this opportunity, for she knew perfectly well that night life was part of my youth, part of my life, ever since I can remember myself. We found the house were my brother-in-law's cousin lived. She was not home but her daughter was and they were expecting us, her mother was at work at some casino, so we were not surprised that she was not home at this hour. Her daughter's name was Betty, she was about seventeen and very nice looking, she received us very warmly and immediately offered us drinks and food. We were so tired from the trip we made, what we all wanted was to go to sleep. To our surprise our rooms were already arranged for us. She said that her mother would arrive at about five to six o'clock in the morning.

When everybody went to their rooms, I stayed behind to ask her a few questions, but to my surprise a young man was at the door. She quickly introduced me to him and said that he was her boy friend, and that they had to go out, that they had a party waiting for them, I excused myself and went to my room.

The next day her mother arrived, her name was, or is, in Gypsy Pabai, which means apple, she was about forty years old and not bad looking. When she saw us she started to cry from happiness. She could hardly speak Gypsy. She apologized and explained that there was nobody to speak with in our language. We talked about everyone who she asked us about, she wanted to know everything, but soon she started to look at her watch, every now and then. We all knew the reason, her daughter did not come home yet, and it was almost nine o'clock in the morning. We had a fast breakfast and before long there was a bottle of whisky on the table, we all knew she needed that drink very badly, so we joined her just to make her feel better. We did not mention her daughter we could see that she was ashamed, but the whisky took its effect, and soon we all started to sing the songs we used to sing in Shanghai, and we all seemed to forget about her daughter. I took her with me to buy some more whisky and also some ready-made food, so that nobody would cook. I went with her to the supermarket because I did not know its whereabouts, and so we drank up to the night, and her daughter still did not appear. She had to go to work and asked us, that is, me and my brother-in-law, to go with her. Of course we said yes. She said that she would put someone else to work for her that night, and that we will come home very quickly. In the casino we took a table and had some drinks, she stood up and went to the waiter who attended us and said something to him, and then she came back to our table. Within ten to fifteen minutes a young girl came, she was very beautiful, she asked her to take her place, and that we were the reason that she could not work, because we were her relatives and came all the way from China to see her. Of course this was a big fat lie, but who cared? We were in a casino and I wanted to have some fun. I asked her to go to play roulette or any other game, but to my surprise she would not let me. I said, "Why?" She said, "You came to see me, or came to lose money?" "Of course we came to see you." "Then let us go home and continue our party." But I knew the real reason she was hurrying home, it was because of her daughter. Although she was high, still she could not hide her worried look. I felt sorry for her. When we arrived her daughter was home, when she saw her she became pale in the face, and without saying a word, went to the telephone. Then Betty cried out, "Mother, no, please, no," but she would not listen, she picked up the phone and dialed a number. "Is this the juvenile delinquent section?" Before she could say anything else, I went up to her and took the phone out of her hand, I said, "Please let us sit down and talk about it, please, for our sake." She looked around on all of us, and said, "This is not the first time that I asked the police to take her away. She is involved in all bad things you can imagine. She practically drove me mad with all the things she has been up to." I poured her a stiff drink, to calm her as much as possible, my sister and my wife took over from there. I spoke to her daughter. I said, "Betty, you must not make your mother suffer so much, she might really go mad, then you will have yourself to blame, you must control your vices." She said. "Thank you for saving me from the cops, I have been there for a few times and it is terrible." She started to cry and went to her room. We drank the whole night. On the next day we all had a big hangover. Later, I invited her and her daughter to have lunch in a Chinese restaurant. Then that night I went to a few casinos, that I promised myself to do, but the incident of the other night did not leave my mind for a long time.

We had to go back to Los Angeles and wait for the ship. In the meantime we decided to look for Gypsies. It was not hard to find Gypsies, all we had to do is hail a taxicab. I told the driver if he knew where Gypsies lived in this city. He said yes. "Please take us to them." He answered, "No trouble." The Gypsies he took us to were from a tribe called Machvaya, they are from Yugoslavia. We came to a big house that looked very expensive, I saw some small boys and girls playing out side the house. I asked one of them to call their elders to see us. Shortly an elderly man came out of the house and said just one word, "Rom?" I said, "Rom." He said, "Please come inside," in Gypsy of course. The house inside was beautiful. Clearly they were very rich. In no time there was food and drinks on the table. Their elders told someone to phone to other Gypsies, in no time the house was full of curious Gypsies. We were asked were we come from. We said, "From China." Of course they asked about our origin. We told them we are Russian Lovara. The elders started to whisper something to each other, then one of them said, "I know very well your tribe, I know them from Russia, I was very young when I met your people. I was about seventeen, that is almost sixty years ago," then he mentioned some names to us which I have heard before. The names were our style of naming our children, like Latsi or Tsino, these are the names of my two sons, at that time my wife was carrying my son Tsino in her womb. When the party got hotter, they started to ask if we had any young girls of marrying age with us. We said no. The man explained, in America we are short of young Gypsy girls, and that the price for a virgin was fifty Mexican gold coins, these types of coins are very expensive in the market. I always knew that they paid in Austrian coins in China. These type of coins are much lighter, and the price was only thirty coins, so they must have been really out of young women in the States. A lot of Gypsies were coming and going, up 'til now none of us spoke English, then one of them said, "Can you speak English?" I said yes, when we started to speak they were taken by surprise, I spoke like they did, even more correctly, they wanted to know how we speak so well. I said, "There are schools in China, too." "Oh, so you are all educated?" I said, "To some degree." One called me aside and whispered in my ear, "You don't have to hide from me, I know you are all from Chicago." I started to laugh. "Why should I do that?" "I don't know, he said, maybe you have something up your sleeve." Then I said, "Can you read?" "Of course I can," he said, looking offended. Then I put my hand in my jacket pocket and took out my passport and showed him my entry stamp in the country. When he saw the proof he instantly blushed. "I apologize," he said. "There is a lot of Gypsies trying to pass for some body else for some reason or another, some come to hide from somebody from other states, who have made trouble there, what made me doubt about you people, because you speak better than we do in English," so we had a drink on that, and that was it. Another one came to me and said that he was interested to give me a job, he was the owner of two middle class hotels, he wanted me because I knew a lot of languages. I politely refused and said that I was about to leave for Brazil.

These Machvaya Gypsies are living mostly of fortune telling, their laws are conservative, but they are changing real fast, they don't dress any more like their ancestors did, they are something like us Lovara, only they still stick to some ignorant customs. The language is quite different from ours, but of course it is understandable. Their women are the bread winners in the family, with some exceptions like the one that owns hotels, some own parking lots, etc., etc., but their women never stop working, they help their husbands even if it's just for expenses, no matter how rich they are. To tell fortune is in their blood, like music in ours.

The ship we sailed on for Brazil was Brazil Maru, a Japanese liner running from Los Angeles to Rio de Janeiro, via the Panama canal to Cristobal, Curaçao, Venezuela and Manaus, that is already Brazil, Salvador, and Rio. The ship was not big, about thirty thousand tons. There were a lot of Japanese immigrants traveling to Brazil. The accommodations were not bad, of course we were on European diet. After a few weeks on the ship, the stench of the Japanese food was almost unbearable, particularly for my wife. She had two months left to give birth to my child Tsino. She constantly felt bad, and some times I took her to the ship's doctor to relieve her vomit. I was eager to get off the ship as soon as possible. Every stop we made, I used to take her ashore, and stay with her there, 'til the last minute of the ship's departure. No, it was not easy, luckily the ship did not roll, otherwise it would have worsened things.

An amazing thing happened in Manaus, Brazil. When we arrived practically all the immigrants were to descend. On the wharf there were a lot of Japanese waiting for the immigrants. To our surprise the Japanese on the wharf were very much darker, than the ones who were descending, and were very poorly dressed, and looked as if they were starved, that made a lot of Japanese cry, including those who were left behind. I had to satisfy my curiosity and asked the officer what was going on? He said that life for the immigrants in the Amazons was not easy, they worked in the interior in large farms owned by the local rich Brazilians, and that they were treated a little less than slaves, and that they had made a contract in Japan that they must stay at the farms for at least five years before they could travel any where else in Brazil. Many died of malaria and other insect bites, at that time communications were poor, the doctors rarely arrived in time to save their patients. While traveling they were full of hope, but when they saw their co-workers on the wharf it was another story. We arrived in Salvador. I decided to leave the ship, we had still about five days to Rio, mostly for my wife's sake. My sister Olga said she would also come with her family. We told the captain that my wife could not take it any more, that we will take a plane to Rio, although I was afraid to fly. But this time was a must, my wife's health was at stake. We had a lot of baggage on the ship, we took with us only what was necessary.

Here in Salvador I saw a lot of pure Negroes working on the wharf, the stench of their sweat was incredible, the whole wharf was invaded by it. I said to myself, "My God, where have I come?" I have never in my life saw so much of colored people. When we went to buy the tickets to Rio the streets were full of them, the town was very dirty, at that time no body spoke in English, we had a hard time to find the tourist office who sold the tickets. Finally we were on the plane, I was very nervous but when the plane took off my nerves subsided. We made just one stop, the city's name is Victoria, by then I was not afraid to fly anymore, it almost seemed fun to me.

And then the big surprise came. Rio was in sight, when I saw the famous Corcovado, the statue of Jesus Christ. I was stunned with the beauty of it and the city below, and the beaches, it was incredible, I have never seen a city so beautiful in my life, my morale was as high as the plane was. Compared with Salvador or any other city this was Paradise, I only prayed that São Paulo was as big and as beautiful as Rio, because our final destination was São Paulo, the reason was that our parents were there, and also we from China pledged to meet in Brazil, São Paulo. We had to wait for the ship to arrive to Rio, so that we may claim our luggage. In the mean time we all went sight seeing. The old city was not so nice, but the new one where the beaches are is something out of this world. The people were very hospitable, particularly to strangers, and were very different from the people of Salvador, I mean in physical appearances. Their skin was much lighter, because they were many mestizos, and you could see a lot of white people on the streets, especially where the beaches are on the south side of the city. I personally fell in love with the city, so did my wife, but my brother-in-law was careful and said, it remains to be seen, if we can work in this country. How wrong I was at Salvador when I regretted to stay in Brazil.

I must explain to my reader that to adapt to any country in the world for a Gypsy is not so very hard because we are used to live in many different countries, as the reader has already learned, and somehow managed to survive. I personally think that we have inherited this ability from our ancestors, and a country like Brazil, I must say, that it was the easiest country that we could get adapted to, as I have already mentioned the people are very hospitable, and you can find here people of all races, like in the USA. In time I was sure that we will learn to live in this wonderful country.

We were in a hurry to get to São Paulo to see our relatives, we have received letters that my sister Lida and her family was on its way to Brazil, but we did not know whether they arrived. My wife was very anxious too, because as my reader already knows, the husband of my sister was my wife's father. When we arrived in São Paulo we had an address of some distant relatives, so we went first to the hotel, left our luggage, and immediately took a taxi to our relatives, to see them, and find out the whereabouts of my sister Lida, and my wife's father and their children, they already had five children. When we finally arrived at their house it was beginning to get dark, their house was very far away from the center, almost on the outskirts of the city. It looked like a very poor section of São Paulo. When we knocked at the door, an elderly woman came out. I immediately recognized her as my father's third cousin. She said, "We were expecting you, please come in." Before I go any further I must explain, that this elderly women was a semi-alcoholic. I say this because I have a reason to say it, unfortunately she sometimes said things she should not say, under the circumstances. We hardly came in the room when she abruptly said, "You heard that your sister died and was

91

thrown in the sea while on their way here." I was completely dumfounded, that feeling I shall never forget, it is impossible to describe. I heard my elder sister scream and run out of the room, my wife followed her and so did my brother-in-law, as for me, I stood there like a statue. After all, my sister Lida was only 38 years old, and had five children and was pregnant with another when I last saw her. 'Til today I don't know how a glass of liquor was in my hand. The old lady said, "Drink this, it will make you feel better." I drank it all and drank again and again. I only stopped two days later when my sister's husband came to take me home.

Later on I found out that she had a miscarriage, and that there was no capable doctor aboard the ship to take care of her. This situation made my sister's husband a very different man. He would shut himself in his room and stay there for days. My wife or my elder sister would bring him some soup and bread for him not to get sick, or even something worse. He only begun to recover when my wife went to the hospital to have my son Tsino. I named him Tsino after my wife's father. This was in 1960. Those were terrible months for all of us. It took a lot of time for him to recover, but thanks to us that we were with him, we did every thing in our power for him to come to, but as the saying goes, time is the best medicine yet invented.

We found a lot of local Gypsies in São Paulo, they were from the Kelderasa tribe, their elders knew personally my grandfather and his family way back from Russia. And there was some Gypsies evacuated from Shanghai, of course we knew them all, so every time some Gypsies visited us, we had to throw a party. It came to such an extent, that we had to hide from them not to drink again, otherwise we were to become alcoholics and, beside we had to find work and quickly.

Thank God this country has a lot of semiprecious and precious stones. We found out that a man in Rio that grew up with us had a big jewelry store, dealing mostly with such stones, his name was Paul Loshnikov, he also was a light weight champion boxer in Shanghai. During the Japanese occupation he was very good-looking, and somehow married the daughter of the president of Pan American airlines. That explained the big store he owned. He was relatively poor last time we saw him, so luck must have come his way. We arrived in Brazil with a reasonable amount of money, so it was easy for us to start any business. Thanks to Paul Loshnikov that we became professionals as far as stones are concerned. We knew a little, but he taught us everything we know today, he even taught us the lapidary arts, and that is not easy. In time me and my wife's father opened a small store in Rio, it was called Vic Mar. We made a lot of money, we bought houses, cars, we did not buy jewels because we made them ourselves. We had our own lapidary business, about ten men worked for us, we bought the latest lapidary tools, this went on for three years.

Maita Vishnevsky and children, Rio de Janeiro. (Photo Victor Vishnevsky.)

Needless to say, life was wonderful in Brazil. My children, I mean Latsi and Zina, were going to school, but Tsino was too small yet to attend school. We lived in a section of São Paulo called Villa Nivi and the house we were living in was ours. For the first time since China we owned our own house and, believe me, it was a good feeling. Our neighbors were all practically Latvians and also Brazilians from the northwest of the country. Later when my daughter Olga was born, in 1965, one of my Brazilian friends in the neighborhood baptized Olga. At that time they used to call us Turks, I don't know why 'til today. The whole neighborhood marveled at the parties we gave, and our close friends were always invited to my parties and also our Gypsy friends in Brazil. I have never felt better than in any other country than Brazil. I loved my wife even more for given me such beautiful children. I was on the way to the top of my profession, what could a person ask for anything more of life? Now my only thought was to give my children the best education that money could buy. I did not want by any means to let my children be like those Gypsies who did not let their children to school for one reason or another, for me the education of my children was my priority in life. Thanks to my father, that he always wanted me to be educated. I know that he did his possible to educate me as far as he could, that is why I know that if there is a place up there where his spirit is, he must be proud of his grandchildren, that thanks to his teachings my children today have a completely different life and for the better. I only wish that my grandchildren will follow their parents' success.

To go on with my story, nature took its course. My wife's father found himself a girl which lived in São Paulo, she was younger than him for almost twenty years, but that did not matter, what mattered, she wanted him all to her self, and that complicated things. So we separated, and besides the business was going slow due to neglect. I opened a gas station in São Paulo. He continued with the lapidary business and was doing fine, but we hardly saw him. He was completely dedicated to his new wife, and to think he almost killed himself for my sister Lida. My children were all going to school and were doing fine, then my wife got pregnant again with my daughter Olga, after five years later of my son Tsino.

Then two tragedies happened. My eldest sister Olga died of an heart attack, and after a month or so my wife's sister Lialia stepped on a rusted nail barefooted and did not go to treat it immediately, but when she went it was already too late, she got blood poisoning from the wound, tetanus. This double tragedy made me very depressed. I did not go to work for three months. I even got sick for a while, but the worse thing was about me, that I left the gas station in the hands of the manager. Taking advantage of my absences, he practically robbed the gas station. I had to start all over again, but what brought up my morale was when I received a letter from my middle sister Zina that she was arriving in Brazil from Iran in a short while. We knew that she got married again, this time to an American sergeant, and was on her way to the US via Brazil to see us. But something happened to their marriage, that up to this day I don't know the real reason of their separation, he even came to Brazil to take her to the States but she would not budge.

I sold the gas station and opened a restaurant with my sister as my partner, serving every thing from hot dogs to hot meals, and drinks of course. For a while everything went just fine, 'til again nature took its course, she met a guy and got married again. He was a good fellow while it lasted, so I decided to leave the joint for them, so they bought me out and that was that.

I as usual went back to my old job dealing in stones. This time I had to travel again but not too far, like Argentina, Uruguay, Chile, Mexico and of course the States. The last two country were far, but profitable. In the States you paid only five percent tax for a carat of semiprecious stones, and that was a good bargain for us who polished stones. By the time my youngest daughter was born, Olga, I named her after my eldest sister, I was doing fine.

Then came the big World's Fair in New York in 1965. Me and my wife's father decided to visit the fair, and also see some friends who evacuated from China, and see if we could open up some new markets. The flight to New York was very bumpy, we had some bad weather, so I suffered a lot. I promised to myself that I will not fly anymore in my life. We went to the fair and that's were I saw my first computer. It was as big as a wardrobe, you paid twenty-five cents to ask a question. I asked a few and it answered me correctly. We stayed in a hotel in Manhattan, we went to see our friends and managed to close a few deals, in the near future, when we had to return. I told my partner that I will not fly back under any circumstances, so we went to look for passenger ships that went direct to Brazil, but unfortunately the date of the passenger ship was very far off, so we went to look around for semi-passenger ships. With luck we found an agency that told us that there was a ship, but not to Brazil but to Peru, which was leaving after two days, there were only twelve cabins. They were already occupied by the share-holders of the company. It was a Vatican-owned line, he explained, and that it was expensive. We told him to wait 'til tomorrow 'til we decide what to do. It took me the whole day and part of the night, to persuade my wife's father to accompany me on that ship. I knew that from Peru there was a bus to Brazil, it was tiresome but to me it was worth a while. The ship was not too big, it made three stops before it reached Peru, the first was Haiti, the capital is Port-au-Prince, in the Caribbean Sea, then to Cartagena, that is Colombia, then we passed the Panama canal, going to Guaya-quil, Equador, that's just before Lima, Peru.

But let me go a little back. When we boarded the ship we found our cabins very well decorated, it looked like a five star hotel, we had a sitting room and a bed room. When I entered my cabin I thought I was ashore, not on a ship. We were supposed to leave before dinner. I took a bath and dressed myself the best I could, because I knew that very important people will be my co-passengers. Then over the microphone the captain announced that we should all assemble in the main hall, he did not say why. When we arrived there were already three to four couples sitting in the hall, most of them were over sixty years old, then two other elderly ladies came in, the captain was right behind them. We all stood up, but the captain quickly told us to be seated. I gathered you here, ladies and gentlemen, to introduce you to each other, we have a long trip ahead of us, the sooner we get to know each other, the better. The first couple he introduced us to was, to my surprise Mr. and Mrs. Nimitz, the ex-commander of the entire US Navy. Admiral Nimitz in person, and his wife. He was not a big man, he had a round face, small eyes and a little on the heavy side, but his presence symbolized authority. When you looked a while in his eyes, and he looked back, you instantly had to look aside, his eyes seemed to penetrate your soul, but his wife was a plump little lady always a smile on her face. The other couple, I don't recall their name, but I do remember his work. He was the chief justice of the Superior Court of New York. The third couple was owners of the du Pont industries. The rest were private millionaires. There was a Jewish couple, they owned a chain of restaurants throughout the states, later he told me he sold them all, only to buy his son a hospital in Miami, only because his son just graduated from a medical university. The two ladies that I mentioned, one was a widow and very rich, the other was a friend she came to accompany her, and the only one that was not rich. I and my wife's father found ourselves between the highest society of the US, but to my surprise in a way they were very simple people, to think that today there is an US navy air craft carrier named after Admiral Nimitz. The captain of the ship usually at dinner would shift us from one table to another so that we should get even more sociable with each other. The food was excellent, the best that money could buy, from lobster to caviar with champagne, and also Chinese food. Each cabin had its turn to buy drinks before dinner for all the passengers, we were about twelve altogether. As I was the youngest of the lot, the widow took a liking to me. She would always find me wherever

I was, and talk to me about everything and everybody. At first I did not mind, but then it was irritating, mostly because I wanted to talk to the Admiral, or the Chief Justice fellow. I was hungry to learn something from these fantastic figures. She would some times write a note, and put it under my door to meet at the bar or some other place. For politeness I went. It was becoming obvious among the passengers that she fell for me, and my partner made jokes about it. Once we were on the deck, I mean the lady and me alone watching the waves of the sea, then I wanted to make a joke, I said to her, "Would you like to be on a raft with Rock Hudson in the sea?" She quickly answered, "I would rather be with you." I looked at her and said, "Are you serious?" She said, "Oh yes, why not?" I quickly changed the subject, and said, "Let's go to the bar and have something to drink." That night I thought to myself, if I would have been a gold digger, this was an opportunity to be a millionaire, she was all alone, her only daughter was married, and came to see her only on Christmas, she did not know that I was married, and up 'til this day I never wear a marriage ring, we Gypsies, the men of course, rarely do, and our women took it for granted.

We stopped at Port-au-Prince, Haiti, we went ashore, of course the widow and her friend accompanied us, we went to see the local market place, it was so dirty that we left as soon as possible. The population of the country is mostly Negro, and there was nothing interesting to see. Of course we had to taste the local drinks, and buy a few things, and that was all. But that night the captain invited some local dancers to make a show for us after dinner, but something funny happened to the dancers. While waiting for us to have dinner, they must have drank a lot of whisky with the waiters. When the show started, the dancers could hardly stand on their feet. The show was a complete flop, the captain asked the head waiter to stop the show. I have never seen anything so disgusting in my life, at the same time I felt sorry for the group, they came to make some money, but after what they have done I very much doubt that they have been paid that night. I felt bad. I know what it is like to be a flop. In my experience as far as shows are concerned, we were always afraid of a flop, every time we went on stage, this is part of show business. But on the other hand it was not their fault exclusively, the waiters should not have given them liquor before the show, but after. But this is life, the dancers were youngsters and free drinks were available, so they took advantage of it.

Our next stop was Cartagena, Colombia. Now here was a lot of things to be seen. This city, the guide told us, was captured for almost twenty times by the pirates, especially by the Blackbeard, the famous pirate of the Caribbean sea. We actually saw the fortresses, which he said were guarding the city from the pirates. Besides there were good emeralds for sale and real cheap, the emeralds of Colombia are the best quality in the world. I and my partner bought to make some jewelry of it when we got home. Then came Panama Canal, we did not even descend because it was so hot. The temperature was over 40 degrees centigrade, so most of us were in our cabins enjoying our air conditioners. Above us was the main saloon hall, which was also air conditioned, so on such hot days we went up there sit around, have a drink.

On one of these occasions I saw the judge sitting alone I came up to him and sat down besides him, then I said to him, "Sir, could I ask you a question?" "By all means," he said. "Do you believe in the death sentence?" "As far as New York is concerned, yes." I asked him this question because I knew that for some time the US did not execute any criminal or political prisoners. "Do you mind if I ask you why?" "Not at all. In New York, as you may know, there are many different nationalities and many poor sections, like Harlem and Greenwich Village, etc., etc., although these people have some help from the social security system, but to cover them all is almost an impossible task, it would bring the local city hall to bankruptcy, and were there is misery there is crime. Recently the statistics showed that assassinations, bank robberies, murders,,etc., etc., were 20 percent higher than last year, and the tourist department informed us, that due to this high rate of criminal activities, the tourists are avoiding New York. They prefer other states, mainly the South, or California and Miami. We have voted this subject a few months ago, but those who were against the highest penalty won." I told him that in Brazil there is no death sentence, but multiple killers were sentenced to even more than a hundred years, he said that he heard about it, he also said the condition of the Brazilian prisons were beyond human comprehension, but in the States it's like a one-star hotel, they have three good meals a day, and also watch a movie every now and then, they constantly take baths and there clothes are always clean because they have their own laundry which they run it themselves, they also work and get paid for it. For those who are for a lesser crime, like theft, fraud, etc., etc,, are taught to have a profession, to find work and be useful to the society when they have served their sentence.

After Panama came Guayaquil, Equador. We wanted to go ashore, but unfortunately there was a big strike going on, the streets were full of demonstrations against the government, it was dangerous. The captain told us that if we want to go ashore we go at our own risk, but on the dock there was a canteen, so we decided to go there and taste the local drinks. Of course the ladies accompanied us. There was a music box there and after a few drinks we even danced. The lady which I referred to earlier got a little higher than usual, and openly tried to kiss me in front of some passengers. I really cannot recall who was there, but I remember that I was embarrassed. I held her off and took her to the chair. When we came aboard the ship I decided to talk to her when she sobers up. That night she did not appear at dinner, her partner must have told her of her behavior. The next morning I saw her standing alone on the far end of the ship. I walked towards her, when she saw me she wanted to run away, but I ran up to her and held her arm. I instantly fell sorry for her. She said, "Please let me go. I made a fool of myself yesterday." Then

I heard me saying, "No, it was not you. Actually it was the local drinks we took, you have not done anything wrong, you have nothing to be ashamed of." Then I thought to myself, these are not the words I wanted to tell her. She started to cry and said, "I am so alone, I need somebody like you to take care of me." "I would very much like to, but you see I am happily married and have four children," then she slowly looked up at me with tears in her eyes, and stared for a few seconds. If that look could kill I would have been dead by now, she pulled her arm away from my hand and ran away. She did not talk to me anymore, it was only two days before we reached the last port, it was Callao, just about fifteen kilometers from Lima, Peru. I and my partner said good bye to everyone except the two ladies. I even did not see them leave the ship. The last words I said to Admiral Nimitz was that we needed men like him in Brazil. I don't know why I said that, maybe because he was such an important man of our times.

We took a few days' rest in Lima, not that we needed it, but just to see the city. We visited the Chinatown of Lima and the food was excellent and cheap. We also saw some of the night life of the city, but it was not too interesting for my taste. Then we visited some jewelry stores, their jewelry rarely contains stones, but they have their own Peruvian style of making jewelry. I found it unique of all South America, their gold is usually of twenty-two carats, and they make art of the gold, they use the art of course of the Inca Dynasty. I could not resist not to buy my wife a beautiful bracelet and earrings, of typical Inca type. I knew she would love it. I have already seen this type of jewelry, our Gypsies in Brazil use it generally when there is a feast, and also gold coins which only Peru produces, and it's the heaviest coin in South America.

The day we went to the bus station, I was shocked to see the condition of the buses. They were very old and in bad condition. I thought to myself, it is more dangerous to travel by them than a plane. My partner made jokes about the buses, he said that they would break down and we would have to walk at least half the way to Brazil. So I had no choice but to fly to Brazil. I remember we took the Braniff airlines. We hardly had any turbulence, only while crossing the Andes mountains we had a little turbulence. The plane passed via Rio and then to São Paulo. He got off in Rio, and I had to fly another forty five minutes to get home, but for the first time in my life I was all alone on the plane, and that made me nervous. I asked a double scotch from the air hostess, and that made me feel better. I was received by my wife and children warmly, as usual.

The first thing I asked my wife, if there was any news about our relatives who were left behind in China? We knew that there were two to three persons who were still in China. To my surprise she said that the ones who were left in China, and we thought the they were dead, were very much alive and were in Europe. When I left them they were teenagers, by now they must be grown-up men. Some Gypsy had come to Brazil from Europe and gave my wife the news, and even an address, they were in Brussels, Belgium. I always wanted to see Europe, so I thought, one day I will visit them.

In the meantime a Russian friend of mine had a luncheonette to sell. He was going to the States and wanted to sell urgently his business, so he offered it to me for a reasonable price. I naturally took advantage of the proposal and bought it. I named it Tata's Place; Tata in Gypsy means father. By now my kids were all in high school, and even the elder ones were working. My son Tsino was helping me to run the place, and of course my wife. I liked the place because practically all the friends of my kids visited the bar, and also many local Gypsies. My wife worked during the day and I used to take over at night. The place was not a gold mine as far as earning is concerned, but it paid my expenses and left a little profit. Besides, I had my job with the stones, not regularly, but it was worthwhile.

That is why I say, that to deal with the Brazilian people is very simple, they are very good people to work with, once you make a friend he stays a friend, at least that's what happened to me. If you ask me where would I want to live the rest of my life, I will tell you Brazil, and believe me I have seen a lot of this world. The Brazilians have a saying that says that God must be Brazilian, because, they argue, that there is no earthquakes, no storms, no twisters, or any other major natural disasters. There are some summer rain floods every now and then, but to such a big country this is nothing. Even in politics they are very flexible. Yes, there is some poverty in Brazil, the famous *favelas* are known throughout world, there is also some corruption, but don't forget that we are considered part of the Third World! There is also lack of work in some places, and also the opposition makes a little noise, but this happens even in the First World! And politics are politics, today the whole world is in a crisis, monetary crises, of course, and even in the First World there are lack of jobs. But I think that by the year 2000 this all will be over, because by that time world will learn how to deal with such crises. This is my opinion, of course. Only when there was dictatorship in the country, I have heard of some violence, but to us strangers nothing seemed different, we worked normally and even earned more. In all my years in Brazil I haven't seen nothing bad, but only good things. Particularly to strangers, they can do anything in their power to help a stranger in distress.

I began to like my work in the luncheonette, mainly because I found new friends and little by little, my place became known by the middle class people, so it became very popular. Only Saturdays we had live music, which my son Tsino organized it, so we had fun and worked at the same time.

Some say that business and fun does not mix, but it was always the other way around with me. While traveling I always mixed fun with business, and it never harmed me, on the contrary it always helped me, as far as morale is concerned. I am a man that always wants people around me, and I love to give parties. My family and the Gypsies who know me know this hobby of mine, so when I throw a party at home, or in a nightclub the sky is the limit. In time I slowed down a little, but nevertheless, on my birthday up 'til today the parties I throw are talked about among my people and my friends. When I was born, my father promised to celebrate the day of my birth as long as he lived, and even to continue after his death, because I was the youngest male child. I had a brother older than me but he died very young, at the age of twenty, this made my father even more determined to keep his promise. So naturally I continue to keep his promise. And to make it even more interesting I was born on the 8th of March, on International Women's Day.

In Brazil my family and I are the only Lovara Gypsies. In Brazil the others who came from China mostly died out. A few are left, but we lost track of them. So I had to mix with the Kelderasa tribe who came from Russia, although their elders mostly died out, so they are considered more Brazilian Gypsies now. I became a godfather to a couple of Kelderasa Gypsies, and I have some prestige among them. I don't want to forget my language, I visit them some times, just to speak with them, and keep my language secure. As far as my children are concerned, only two of them speak well, that is, Latsi, the eldest, and Olga, the youngest, but all of them understand every word I say. Zina and Tsino speak only when its absolutely necessary, but I don't blame them, they are married to Brazilians, and also their work keeps them out all day. And besides, all my children finished Brazilian universities. Thank God my children are all well-to-do and happily married. They don't mix with any local Gypsies, mainly because the standard of education is different. In any case they have a certain friendship with the Gypsies that are my friends, as I have with their friends. One thing, I am proud of my children, they never deny their nationality, they always say that they are Gypsies, and that they are proud of it.

We even have a church in Brazil, somewhere in the town called Campinas, in São Paulo state. I never visited it because I am a Catholic, and the church in Campinas belongs to Billy Graham's organization, the famous pastor of the USA. Of course there are exceptions. I was invited a number of times to visit the church, but I politely declined, but they insist. Every now and then when we meet at weddings or any other events they always invite me, but to no avail. Their church does not allow them to drink liquor, but almost everyone does it. All of them came from Europe. Some pastors had relatives living in Brazil, so they came over and started to preach exclusively to Gypsies. The same thing happened throughout the world, it spread like wild fire in the forest. Some are so fanatic that they don't serve liquor even on their own weddings, they serve tea with cakes, and of course the wedding cake. But the youngsters usually go around the corner and drink without being seen. I never went and never will go to such a wedding, even if it would have been my brother's. Now

I hear that things are being declined, due to the severe pressure of the church. It is, I think, becoming too radical for Gypsies to withstand it. I personally don't like to be pushed around by any institution, whether it's a church or anything else. I believe in God as a Catholic like my forefathers did, and I follow their example.

There are Gypsies in Brazil that have come to Brazil hundreds of years ago, they are mostly living in the north part of Brazil. They have completely forgotten to speak in our language, but they still hold on to some traditional customs, living in tents. Their work is trading horses or mules, and also working with copper, making pots and other cooking items. They are very ignorant. Their children practically don't go to schools, mainly because they don't stay in one place for a long time. They still buy their women, but instead of gold, they deal in horses or mules. These are the most backward Gypsies I have ever seen, but still when you say that you are a Gypsy you get an utmost respect.

This is an ever-changing world, the Gypsies today are very different than, let's say, a half a century ago, they are more materialistic and give very little respect to their elders. We still have our courts of justice. Our courts of justice are always controlled by our elders. When someone has something against the other he or she asks the elders to unite in a saloon for many people to hear about the case. But rarely they are obeyed, unless the person involved is threatened with violence or the local police, then he pays whatever he owes. To go to the police and denounce a Gypsy was a shameful thing once upon a time, because we believed in our justice. But today all is almost gone, and not only in Brazil but through out the world. The only things that did not change much, is our weddings, our music, our dancing, and the most important, our spirit to live, and travel as much as possible, and of course our freedom.

In Brazil we found a lot of White Russians who lived mostly in São Paulo. They were from China of course. These were our close friends, two couples who always owned nightclubs in China. They opened a nightclub in São Paulo which was called

Balalaika. They were Russian Jews, and also knew all my family from top to bottom. We always reserved tables there for New Year's or other feasts. When we went there we had to play some Russian Gypsy music for them. They used to join us at the table and drink with us 'til the morning. When we were together it reminded us of China, and the good times we used to have there, and of course their youth—they were much older than I was for at least fifteen years. Both couples were childless. Unfortunately they had some trouble with the local income tax bureau, and they sold the restaurant to a Gypsy friend of ours who was also from China. But he was a sick man and could not run the restaurant. I wanted to buy the joint but I was in a different business. I had to travel a lot, so the only Russian nightclub in São Paulo closed down. Since then there were a couple of joints, but nothing compared to Balalaika, and today there is not a single one, mostly because the Russian immigrants, not only from China, but throughout the world, re-immigrated to the States, and the elder ones died out. Once in São Paulo there were a lot of Russians, they even had their own settlement called Vila Zelina. Almost all of them lived there, it was like little Russia. This was in the sixties, but today there are few families left. Now who took over the zone are mostly Brazilians who came from the north to run away from the dry climate, it hardly rains up there. As a matter of fact, only in São Paulo there is said to be three million people from the north. Today São Paulo is completely different than I used to know.

I have said earlier in my book that there were two relatives of mine living in Belgium, they were the last Gypsies evacuated from China. So I decided to visit them on my vacation. My children were no more children any more, they were all working and almost self-sufficient. Only my daughter Olga accompanied me and my wife. When we arrived there we were very happy to see them, because these relatives we have not seen for nearly thirty years. They were the ones who informed us that in Stockholm, Sweden, we had hundreds of relatives, that I have never seen in my life, both from my mother's side, and father's side. I remember their names, but to see them was another story. I was told by my parents that they were all left behind in Soviet Russia, but somehow they ran away from Russia to Poland, and were now in Stockholm, so I wanted to see them by any means.

But before going there, I also had a cousin in Paris who grew up with me in China, and worked in a Russian nightclub by the name of Moscow. She and her husband which was not Gypsy, but passed for one, performed there. Since Paris was not far from where we were we decided to go to see her. We took a train. In a few hours we were in Paris. I immediately liked Paris, because the buildings and houses reminded me very much of Shanghai's French Concession where I grew up. Although we had her address, we did not go to her at once. We wanted to surprise her, going to her nightclub. We went to a hotel, and prepared ourselves to paint the town red that night, with my cousin of course. I remember I asked the waiter what time the night life starts. He said that depends were we want to go. We told him about the Russian nightclub which was called Moscow. He said he will find out in a minute. When he came back we were surprised to hear him say that the nightclub would start at eleven PM, so that gave us considerable time to kill. We went sightseeing and, believe me, Paris is really what the romantic poets say to be, the air inspires romance, at least that's how I felt, or was it my imagination? We visited the Eiffel Tower, which I considered it a must. Naturally we visited some museums at the request of my daughter, because I personally don't understand too much about art, especially modern art, but I do appreciate the Mona Lisa of Da Vinci, and Van Gogh, etc., etc. But what I was longing for is to see my cousin's show, and after that have fun as much as possible.

That night we dressed to kill and took a taxi towards the Russian club. I remember we arrived at midnight, we entered the club, the waiter assisted us to the table, and then brought us the menu. The place was nicely decorated typical Russian style, the waiters were all dressed like old-style Russians do, it was all colorful and cheerful. The only thing that bothered me was the musicians, the youngest of them was over sixty years old, imagine the rest? We did not order food, just *zakuska*, which means salt fish or salt vegetables, like the famous Russian cucumber, that only goes with vodka, this is not considered food, but just to break the taste of the vodka. For my daughter I ordered Russian wine. The show did not begin yet, I was thrilled to know that we did not miss anything. I was a little nervous, I wondered how she was dancing now? After all, on the road to freedom from China, she was just a kid, about fifteen years old. My sister Lida taught her all she knew about dancing Gypsy-style, of course, and we used to rehearse for hours at a time, for her to make the right steps. But now she was considered a star in that nightclub. Before entering we saw her photograph at the entrance, announcing her as the main event. After a couple of drinks I calmed down. The place was getting fuller every minute that passed, until there were practically no tables, and then the show started. I was surprised to see the waiters bring in a large table, and put it in the middle of the dancing floor, and surrounded it with chairs. Then they brought a lot of lighted candles and put it on the table, then the lights went out. I saw ten to twelve women and men come and sit around the table, all dressed in Russian costumes, then the music started and they began to sing as a chorus. I was stunned by the beautiful melody, and the lyrics of the song was something I did not hear for decades. It moved me very much. By the time it was over, I had had two extra drinks and my wife was in tears. Then they announced a couple of Bulgarian dancers that I did not appreciate. I was waiting for the big moment, and was beginning to feel high. When they announced her name as the Gypsy Zina Vishnevsky, the whole nightclub became silent. I was proud that she still used our surname, although she was married to an Armenian. She came out on the dancing floor as a big star should, all these years have given her experience. There was no doubt about it, the applause she received proved it, she danced our Gypsy dance with all her spirit and grace, although she was over fifty, but she still radiated her youth that I knew. When she finished the applause was even louder, then she was gone. I asked the waiter if I could go backstage. I explained that she was my cousin, but the waiter said he will tell her and she might come to see us herself.

We waited for a few minutes, and then I saw her coming towards us. In the next few seconds I cannot explain what happened, she just stood there very pale, and I thought she would collapse any second, but I quickly stood up and held her by the hand. I pulled a chair for her to sit down, she was sobbing like a child, slowly she regained her self-control. "Who is this beautiful young woman? She must be your youngest daughter." "Yes," I said. "This is Olga." She kissed my daughter's forehead, and said, "I want to hug you all, but this is not the place to do it, instead let's all have a drink. When we finished having the drink," she said, "I also want to ask you a million of questions, but this we will do at my home after I am finished here." Then she called the waiter and said something in his ear, the waiter nodded and went away. I said that I wanted to see her husband. "Later," she said. "I have to go now, please don't go away, it seems like a dream to see you again." Her second show was with her husband. They were both dressed Gypsy-style, they looked very beautiful. Her husband surprised me. He looked much younger than my cousin and very handsome. They sang a Russian Gypsy song, doing a duet. The song they sang was not familiar to me, it must have come from Russia recently. I know because I have a collection of old and new records, not complete of course, but wherever I hear a Russian Gypsy song that I don't have, I try my best to have it. That night, as I wanted to pay the bill, the bill was already paid. I think that's what she whispered in the waiter's ear. She did what she promised, we went to her apartment and drank 'til the morning. We sang our old hits, we talked about everything and everyone.

When I asked about our relatives in Stockholm, I was surprised to hear that she already has been there, and confirmed what my two relatives in Belgium said. She said that there were so many, that she did not have time to see them all. When we parted we promised to be in touch at all times. She also gave us an address who is our direct relative in Stockholm. Then without warning she said, "You must first visit Hamburg, Germany, because," she went on to say, our first cousin by the name of Hanny was living there. She also said that if we bypass him he will get upset, after all he was the son of my father's brother, and very famous throughout Europe. I have never seen him, so we decided to visit Hamburg. First we traveled by train to our destination in Germany. Of course we telephoned to him before embarking on the train. My cousin Zina telephoned him personally from the railway station in Paris to meet us on our arrival.

We were met by about ten people, I instantly recognized my cousin, he looked very much like me or my other cousins. We embraced and even kissed each other like the Russians do, his wife and daughters were also present and also his son-in-laws. The cars they owned were all Mercedes-Benz, the most expensive type, and when we arrived we saw instantly that they were well to do. The table was already waiting for us, there were other Gypsies who also were invited to see us. On the table were three different types of drinks, Russian, German, and French. The food was all homemade, and we loved it because it had that Gypsy taste that only a Gypsy knows. He told me that he was in the carpet business, and that mostly all the Gypsies in Germany did the same.

He showed us some photos of my father and his father, and also our grandparents. His eldest daughter, by the name of Mimi, looked so much as my sister Lida who died on the ship, and I told him so. Then he said the apples on a tree, when they fall, they don't fall far away from the tree. You don't have to be clever to understand what he meant by that, obviously we are from the same tree.

As usual we had a wonderful time. I told him that my destination was Stockholm. He advised me to hire a car to travel to Stockholm, because this time of the year the country side is beautiful. Besides, we will need a car to see just a part of our relatives, and they live far away from each other. We stayed three more days in Hamburg before we started our journey again. We traveled by car 'til the edge of the Baltic sea, there we boarded a luxury ship, which you could take your car along, that takes you to Gothenburg, Sweden. On board we had a good time, there was a nightclub and also a casino where we gambled a little, there was even a floor show which we enjoyed very much. But the trip was very short, not even twenty-four hours. From Gothenburg to Stockholm was about six-hundred kilometers by car, but we had no regrets, we loved every minute of it.

Again my relatives knew about my arrival, they were informed by my cousin in Hamburg by telephone. This time they did not know when we will arrive, because we were by car, but when we did arrive we had a very hard time finding them, although we had the address, but it was some were on the outskirts of Stockholm. But when we did find them it was the wrong place, they were also related to us, but from very far and they were also Lovara as we are. They told me that my third cousin was living here before, but had moved very recently. It was very late at night by now so they insisted for us to stay. They had a very nice apartment and one room was available, so we had no choice but to stay. In that apartment only a woman and her son were living. She was divorced and about thirty-five years old, and was called by the name of Kookla, which means a doll in Russian. Her son's name was Derek, he was about twenty years old. There was no one else, as I already said. It was quite late. We went to bed because we were very tired. She also knew that we should arrive, so there were no surprises. By morning the whole Gypsy clan knew of our arrival, she must have telephoned them while we were still asleep.

We had hardly had our breakfast when our relatives began to arrive. Even those who worked gave some excuse to their bosses, just to come and see us. Every one of them brought a bottle of some kind of liquor with them, and also some food to go along with it, but my host did not like the idea. But as she was a woman and divorced, they asked her not to take this act into consideration, but she still went out and brought her own drink and food. It came to such an extent that there was no more place on the table. Then came the music instruments. When they started to play I was stunned, and to think that I considered myself a musician, these people were professional, no wonder the communist regime had given them permission to leave, because they were so good and were entitled to be seen by the world.

Earlier I promised my reader that I will explain how I got to know that we Gypsies are from India. These were the people who were invited by Indira Gandhi, the ex-Prime Minister of India to come to Bombay for a music festival, and, as I said earlier in this book, Prime Minister Indira Gandhi confirmed that we Gypsies are her people, and that we left India hundreds of years ago, 'til today nobody knows why.

The music they played made me want to cry. I hardly could control myself. My wife was crying openly. These songs were played by my father on a Russian type accordion, and he was good at it too, when he was younger of course. When I bought my first piano accordion he was the one that taught me my first song. We all played by ear, never by notes, but these people, they could play symphony by notes.

We were already in high gear when my third cousin arrived. There were so many people that they had to indicate me to him by finger. He came to me with tears in his eyes—this cousin was the sentimental type, unlike the other in Hamburg. They gave him a place to sit beside me, so that we would get more acquainted. To my surprise he did not drink hard drinks. I asked him why. He said he was suffering from diabetes. He was only a few years older than I was. Then he said, "You have come to the wrong place." I said I knew about it. Then he said, "By all the rights you should stay at my place." I said to him not to worry about it, after all this woman whose guest I was is also our far relative. He wanted to say something, but I stopped him politely. "We will talk about this later, lets enjoy the party. Don't forget this party is for my honor." He said, "You are right, have fun and enjoy your party." To my surprise he excused himself and left. Then someone told me that after he got sick, he stopped participating in any festival events. I felt sorry for him but what to do, life is such.

That day was just a sample, every other day I was invited to a party in my honor. Only once I had time to go downtown to a Chinese restaurant and invited my host and other near relatives. We went to the Chinese restaurant because I knew how to order Chinese dishes that they never even heard of, and they enjoyed watching me speak Chinese. They adored the food, I ordered dishes they have never tasted anything like this before. They told me that in Russia I had even more relatives than in Stockholm. I wanted to go and see them, but it was a communist country, although it changed somewhat, but only God knows how much.

While we were at the restaurant, I took a chance to go out and buy my airplane tickets for home, so I took a young man who knew his way around the center of the city, so that he may find me a tourism agency. Luckily there was a travel agency near by, so we entered. I did not need him to translate for me, because the young beautiful girl spoke fluently English. I told her that

I wanted three tickets for São Paulo Brazil. She offered me a few options I considered very expensive. I asked her if she could find me a less expensive airline, she said that she will find out in a minute or so, and so she did, she said that the less expensive airline was the Russian Aeroflot, but the only catch to it was that it did not stop in Brazil, but in Argentina. The difference of the price was almost forty percent less, but what I liked about the route was that the plane had to stop in Moscow for thirty hours, we had to change planes there. But there was another surprise for us, we had to stay at the hotel which the airways provides, and could not leave the hotel 'til we change planes. But what picked up my hope was when she added that we might have a tour of the city on a bus, but she could not guarantee us this privilege. I told her to issue the tickets. The flight was scheduled two days from now. I was delighted just to think that I will be visiting a country, which my father and forefathers lived in Moscow at least a century ago, just to think of it made my skin crawl.

Then something strange happened, when we arrived home I received a phone call from my cousin, the one who left me at the party, what he told me I could not believe my ears. He said that there are rumors that someone of our clan, he does not know who, wants to abduct my daughter, I was stunned. These type of acts are no news to me, we Lovara have this habit. I thanked him for his information, as a matter of fact I myself have abducted my wife Maita, but that was another story. My reader remembers about it, in the earlier pages of this book. That made me tell my wife, and my host. My host tranquilized me by saying that we are not in a jungle, the old days are gone, there are laws that punish very severely for such acts, and even a child knows that. Besides, my son Derek and his cousins will watch over Olga until you leave. Then Olga said, "Just let them try, we shall beat the hell out of them, whoever they are." But I could see that my wife was worried, and so was I, but not as much as I was a half an hour ago. This time a few families together were giving me a farewell party. This party I shall never forget. Almost the whole clan was present. There were two accordions, several guitars, and singers. To me this was Paradise, the climate was of sheer happiness. I was supposed to take the plane at ten in the morning, we drank from four in the afternoon 'til seven o'clock in morning, so I had only three hours to go. I was high and even wanted to change the tickets, but my wife talked me out of it. They took me all to the airport and even there we had some drinks, we were so many that the whole bar was occupied by us. They stayed till the last minute, the parting was very sad, we all were crying openly. People stared at us, but we did not seem to care. Almost all of them asked me to come back again, as it seems I and my family was a complete success with my relatives.

The two-hour or so flight to Stockholm I don't remember, I slept all the way.

When we arrived I felt the hangover overtaking me. We had to wait two hours before it was our turn at the immigration. There was no bar. We were all thirsty but we did not dare to drink from the tap water in the toilets, which were very dirty for an airport of that magnitude. It was very hot, about thirty centigrade. We were in the plain summer in Russia, it was August, the hottest month in Moscow. I was wearing dark glasses mostly because I had the hangover. When I showed my passport to the officer, even before opening it he asked me to take off, my glasses with a voice that seemed to me very offensive, and in very bad English. I nearly cursed him in Russian, but then I restrained myself, after all this was a communist country, and these people are unpredictable.

They took us to building not too far away from the airport. When we entered in the building I was surprised to see so many Indians, who have also arrived the same time from some city of India. There were all Russian young girls trying to accommodate us to our rooms, but they had a hard time with the Indians, who only spoke in English, and the poor Russian girls could not understand them very well. The first thing we did when we arrived was to quench our thirst in the local bar. There were about twenty or more Indians ahead of us, with a lot of children of all sizes. One Indian family with about three children were trying to tell the Russian girl that they needed more mattresses for the children, but the girl was telling them that at the moment they were out of mattresses, and that they have sent for some, it will arrive in a few hours, but the Indian did not seem to understand. Up 'til now I did not speak a word in Russian, but seeing how the young Russian girl suffered I decided to go to her aid and serve as an interpreter. Later I regretted the action that I took. It took me hours before I was released of my burden, but in compensation I was treated like a VIP. We got the most comfortable room. They even brought us soap, which we did not use because we always carried our own, and besides their soap was of a very bad quality. Even tea was served in the room which no other passenger had that privilege.

When we went to dinner which the airline company offered for our delay, the food was inedible cold *borsht*, that is the famous Russian cabbage soup, and some rice with a few meat balls with black or white bread. By now almost the whole building knew that I spoke in Russian I called the waitress and politely said that I would like to order my food and pay for it, and asked her to bring the menu. Instead she brought the cook. The man said that they had no menu available, that the food was the same for all passengers. Before I wanted to say anything he added, "But for you we will make an exception, but unfortunately we have very little options, we could offer you a good steak with french fries, or a hamburger with some vegetables. Oh, and I can arrange some Russian caviar if you wish." I asked my wife and daughter what they wanted. We all decided for the steak, and the caviar to go with it. I don't remember how much I paid for it, but I know it was very cheap in, dollars of course.

The funny thing about the building was, that every plane that had to overnight there had its own floor, and could not mix with others. The elevator had the number of your flight written over the button of the elevator, the others were all covered. There was always a young girl beside the elevator to ask which flight you were on, so that she may change the number. We could only mix in the dining room.

Before going to bed I had a phone call from the manager of the building, she asked to come down, I was surprised at such a late hour, I did not know what to think, I admit I was a little scared. When I came to her office she asked me to sit down politely, then said, "I asked you to come down at this hour, because I want you to be the first one on the list for the excursion to Moscow tomorrow, you don't want to lose it do you?" I did not know how to thank her. When I was about to go she asked me, "By the way, what is your destination?" I said, "Brazil." She said, "Lucky you." The airport was at the outskirts of the city, it was not the main international airport. When we were about to get on the bus we were all told not to use our photograph cameras. Only when we reach the city we will be told when and were we could photograph. We waited for our guide to come who spoke fluently English. When she arrived then we began our journey to Moscow. On the way I saw a lot of food factories, but they were all foreign of the ex-communist bloc. The day was very beautiful. There was practically no smog, the reason for that was obvious, there were very little cars on the road and even in the city. We visited the Red Square. I remember our guide explained that it was called the Red Square, not because, like most people think, that a lot of blood was spilled here during the Revolution, but Peter the Great, the famous Tsar, had named it that way, but she did not say why. We also visited the largest hotel in the world, she said it contained a thousand rooms. The Lenin's mausoleum was a must, but we were not allowed to go off the bus. She told us we could take photos of it. And then we took a lot of photos, the Kremlin, the statue of Karl Marx, etc., etc., but all through the window of the bus.

Then what caught my eye was when we crossed a bridge below us, it was the river Moskva Rech, the famous river that I have seen a movie about, it runs right through the city. It was a hot day, there were thousands of white bodies on the bank of the river taking a sunbath. The women wore bathing suits which were in style a couple of decades ago, it was a very poor sight, compared to the beaches of Rio de Janeiro. I felt sorry for these Russian women, because they did not have a chance to show their beauty, and believe me the Russian women are beautiful.

When we arrived back to the building, I regretted that I did not filed for a visa in Stockholm to spend a few days in Moscow, but then I thought, after the ten days that I passed drinking in Stockholm, in Moscow it could have been worse. I was afraid that I might turn to be an alcoholic. These people don't take no for an answer. If you refuse to join them for a drink, if you insist not to drink, the first thing they ask you if you are sick? You say, no I am not sick, then drink with us, otherwise you offend us, after all it is for your health and prosperity, so you just can not refuse. Besides, they drink Russian style, they call it bottoms up.

As a matter of fact the Swedish people don't seem to know how to drink. The proof of that is that they do not sell liquor on working days. And also, when you go to a restaurant they will sell you only one drink and you have to order food with it! Otherwise they will not sell you that single drink, that's the government's orders.

My people in Stockholm drink, particularly the young people, but not to an extent to be alcoholics. There are exceptions, of course, like in any country in this world. It's only that our parties are more musical, our dancing is part of our culture, that is why throughout the centuries we are known to be musical people and have the most happiest parties that I ever came across. One has to see one party, or a wedding of our Gypsy people, to believe it. It's our nature that is like that, we don't have to use liquor to sing or dance, to us it comes naturally.

I used to do that when I was much younger. In Brazil I have learned to drink moderately. This type of drinking was out of the question, as far as I was concerned, but still to sit and drink the whole night, even moderately, you get drunk, but they did not seem to understand that. I think that the climate has something to do with their drinking, because in Stockholm is mostly cold, only a few months are warm, and besides they are all mostly musicians, and live more during the night than the day, of course I refer this all to the younger of the clan, their elders almost don't drink.

So I said to myself some day I shall return, and I still say it up 'til today if God permits. The next day early in the morning we were taken to the airport. We had time to go to the free shop. We bought a samovar, which is a traditional Russian water boiling device. We also bought some paintings of famous Russian painters, not the original of course. We bought some records of Russian Gypsy music, and some Russian-made dolls made out of wood, and other gadgets. Then the hostess asked us to follow her to the plane.

This plane was different from the one we arrived with, it was much larger and looked a little tired. We entered in the plane by its belly, which made me even more surprised, traditionally you enter on the side of the plane. The plane inside was very poorly decorated, and half of the seats were sealed off, which made me feel even more worried. There were about fifty to sixty passengers. My wife sensed my worry, and said, "Please don't get nervous. God is good. He will take us home safely." We waited for about twenty minutes and nothing happened, even the other passengers were restless, they were all mostly Argentinians. When the hostess came and brought us tea, I asked her what was the delay. She said that some twenty-odd passengers were about to arrive. She was surprised that I talked to her in Russian, she said, "It is very nice of you to talk to me in Russian. You might be a help to us, because there are a lot of Latin American passengers which don't speak English, and you could translate for us, of course if you wish." I said, "I will be honored."

The twenty-odd passengers finally arrived. They were all young people, and all were male and half drunk, the seats that were sealed off was reserved for them. They accommodated themselves very well, because even before the plane started to roll half of them were asleep. I was anxious to know were this youngsters came from, because the language they spoke among themselves was not Russian. A couple of them were sitting behind my seat. We were less then an hour in the air when one of them from behind of my seat leaned over to talk to me. He said, "Señor, can I speak to you a moment?" His English was very bad. "Yes," I said. "I wish you do me a favor." I said, "If I can. What is it you want?" "Sir," he said, "we are all sailors, we come from Lithuania, now we are going to Dakar, Senegal, Africa, to change the crew which is going on vacation. We drank a little vodka on the train coming to Moscow, so I need a drink very much. Please, if you can, buy me a small bottle of vodka. You see, we are not allowed to buy vodka on the plane, they gave the order to the captain of the plane, do me this favor, please." Then he took some coins out of his pocket, and trying to give it to me. I said, "No money. I will buy you the vodka and with my money, but you must wait because the hostesses are always going up and down, they might get suspicious and I might also get in trouble." "Thank you, thank you very much." Then I asked, "Do you speak in Russian?" He said yes. "So let's speak in Russian, so that the hostesses will not get too suspicious. If they hear that we speak Russian among ourselves they will think that we are making friends." My wife, as usual, protested, she spoke in Gypsy of course for the sailor not to understand. I said for her not to worry, that I myself will not have a drop. After a few minutes I stood up and went where the hostesses are preparing the food and drinks. I asked if they had vodka to sell. One of them said yes. I quickly explained that I forgot to buy the vodka in the free shop. "Oh," she said, "don't you worry. We have several types of vodka, it is only for you to choose, and there are also many other typical Russian items." I said, "I want the best brand of vodka." She said, "Yes, of course." I bought four bottles and also some chocolates. When I came back to my seat I slowly slipped a bottle to the sailor.

All this situation distracted my attention from the flight we were taking, and it was a surprisingly smooth flight with practically no turbulence. I felt fine. We were going home and I was happy.

In the following lines something very funny happened to me. I gave my seat to my daughter so that she might feel more comfortable. There was an empty seat just across the sailor to whom I provided the vodka. He seemed very pleased that I came more near to him so he could talk to me. Every now and then he would put his head down and take a shot of the vodka, of course when the hostess was not around. He was the only one of his crew that did not sleep. I was getting tired of his talk, and he was steadily getting more drunk. I began to regret that I bought him that bottle of vodka. Then he started to criticize the Russians, who he said that they occupied his country, and did not even let him drink when ever he wanted to. He only stopped talking whenever the hostess passed by to bring us tea or something to eat. He used the tea as a chaser to wash down the vodka. About three seats in front of us there was a man with a small boy. The man was very well dressed. Every now and then he also ducked his head. I thought he must be doing the same thing the sailor did. Once I passed by him and saw that the boy was fast asleep, but I saw the bottle. For curiosity I asked the hostess who the man was. She said that he was a Russian diplomat, taking the son of the Ambassador to Argentina for vacation, so I thought there were two drunks aboard.

A few times the hostess came to me to read a bulletin for the Latin Americans who did not speak English about the planes altitude, and at what time we will arrive in Budapest, etc., etc. Those who were awake were interested, the rest were fast asleep and so was my family.

What worried me was the two drunks, before long when all was very quiet. To my despair the diplomat stood up and slowly made his way to us, and gently said, "Can I join you, gentlemen?" I said, "By all means." I stood up and gave him my seat, but he protested, and said, "Don't leave us, have a drink with us." I answered, "No, thanks. I don't drink because I am taking medicine. I lied. So I went to sit a few seats further from them. Soon they began to talk and drink and forgot that I even existed.

I was almost asleep when I heard that there was a quarrel going on behind me. When I turned around I saw the sailor stand to his feet and then punch the diplomat right on his chin. I got there as fast as I could to separate the fight. When I got between them, this time the diplomat was on his feet and threw a punch. As I was between them I got the punch that was meant for the sailor, but fortunately not in the face but on my chest, since he was much shorter than I am. Then the hostess ran up and said, "What is going on?" I said, "Nothing, we are just changing seats." Apparently she did not see the fight, she only said, "Please be more quiet." The diplomat went back to his seat and I went to mine, but I saw that the diplomat was bleeding from his mouth slightly.

When we reached Dakar, Africa, we all were asked to leave the plane. I was curious and asked the hostess why. She said we had to change planes here. We all went to a restaurant. When we sat down, the diplomat came up to me and said, "Can I speak with you for a moment in private?" I said, "Yes, of course." He took me aside and said, "I apologize for what had happened on the plane." I said, "Don't think about it, it was not you, it was the vodka." We shook hands and I went back to my table. My wife asked what the man wanted. "Oh," I said, "there was some misunderstanding on the plane." I quickly added, "Not with me, but my friend the sailor, there nearly was a fight between them, and I stopped it." "You see," she said, "you should have not given him the vodka." It was three o'clock in the morning in Dakar, the free shops were mostly closed, but still we managed to buy some remembrances.

We arrived in Buenos Aires safely. I even enjoyed the flight. These Russian planes might look old, but they fly very smoothly. We changed planes again and in two hours time we were back home.

The first thing I did was to telephone to my sons and daughter. The very same night we gathered together, my son Latsi, his wife Regina, his three daughters, Jessica, Karina, and Nataly, my second son's family, Tsino, his wife Rosy, his son Victor, named after me, and his small daughter Irene, then comes my daughter Zina, her husband, Antonio Carlos Kohn—for short we call him Tais—an incredible human being. I said that because he adapted to our way of life very quickly, and, among other things, I consider him like my son, as I do the other son-in-law. Tais is from a German descent, and his mother, Italian. We all call her Beba, don't ask me why. And their daughter, Stephanie. This meeting was like a party, everybody wanted to know about our relatives in Europe. We talked almost up 'til dawn. Of course my wife was the orator for me and my daughter Olga.

Then I asked what news they had for us. To my surprise they told me that our two relatives that I met in Belgium were here in São Paulo. One of them was courting my wife's auntie, the other was also courting a Gypsy woman. They came here specifically to get married to Gypsy women. They found out through me that these women were available, so they did not think twice. They were both well over forty years old, the women that I just mentioned were in their late thirties, and to my surprise it worked. The one that was my wife's auntie eloped with her husband, but the other came to me for help as the eldest of the clan. I was asked to ask for her hand from her mother, and so I did, since she was divorced and with a son of about five years old. Her mother quickly agreed. I did everything in my power to help him in any way I could, because his father and mine were third cousins, I even became the godfather of his son, and 'til today I help as I can when he needs it.

My wife's auntie, one of the twins that I mentioned earlier in my book, by the name of Lola, who eloped, she traveled all the way to Macao, China, because her husband's sister was living there with her sons and daughters. Later her auntie wrote us a letter inviting us to come and see them. It is not too easy to invite anybody halfway around the world, but it seemed to me he was doing fine in his store in Macao, selling imported things. I certainly loved the idea to see China after all these years, it was very tempting. They wanted our reply in a month or so, because at that time they will have their vacation. I talked to my wife over and over again about the trip, but she would not budge, and she had a good reason for it. My daughter Olga, the youngest, was about to get married, but my daughter wanted to graduate from the university first, and become a lawyer. Then, and only then, she would get married. So we had to write a letter and tell them that only after a year or so we could accept their invitation.

In the mean time I opened a videotape store, which I put my daughter Olga to be in charge. She worked and studied very hard. I also did what I could to help her, but she knew the business more than I did and was good at it, too.

So time came and finally she graduated to become a lawyer. I and my family are to this day very proud of her. As a matter of fact she is still studying, this time to be a judge. The man whom she was about to marry had already his lawyer's office, a good working man. A fanatic for the São Paulo football team, he would sometimes take a plane to another city were his team played, just to watch it for ninety minutes. This I would never understand, I don't like to be radical on sports, or politics, but very rarely, where my family is concerned. You have to be radical on some issues, maybe it is my age. I admit that in time I have changed, as a matter of fact everything changes in the long run, all you have to do is look at yourself in the mirror in the morning, and you have your answer. Finally the time was set for them to get married. It was a nice wedding, and we sent them off to their honeymoon in Cancun, Mexico.

So me and my wife are all alone in the big house that was once filled with children. This is life, maybe God meant it that way. To escape this loneliness I immediately sent a cable to my wife's auntie, and asked if the invitation to see them in China was still available. The reply came almost immediately. They asked us to go to the Korean airlines, and said that our tickets will arrive there in a few days. I was delighted by their generosity, but I wanted something more. I wanted to see again Japan. I never saw Korea, as it was en route, why not see it, too? There was also Taiwan, Malaysia, Singapore, and Bangkok, Thailand.

When I went to receive the tickets, I added all these countries into it. Of course, I paid the difference. Our route was São Paulo, New York, then Anchorage, Alaska, then direct to Tokyo, Japan. I will never forget what I have seen in Anchorage. We stopped there to take fuel. In the hall of the airport's restaurant we saw a big stuffed white Alaskan bear. He or she stood about three feet high, on his feet of course, it seemed so lifelike that it scared me and my wife. There were also wolves and other animals of the region. They were selling women's over' coats of chinchilla fur, and also mink furs that cost a fortune. I wanted to buy myself a simple skin jacket, only the collar was made out of some type of fur. When I asked the price, I was stunned, it was two thousand dollars. What we bought was some red caviar, and also smoked salmon fish.

When we arrived in Tokyo, I was completely surprised. It has changed, I only recognized Ginza, that's the center of the city, the rest was all new. After all, almost thirty years has passed, the last time I passed from here. Not only the city have changed, but also the people. To me the people have become more aggressive, the politeness of the Japanese people has practically diminished, as far as foreigners are concerned. In the 'sixties a foreigner was respected, you were received very well wherever you went. Their hospitality has gone. They reminded me of the proud Japanese warriors in Shanghai, for whom you sometimes had to bow when you had to cross their path. Between them they seemed polite and bowed to each other. I thought to myself that their prosperity has gone up to their heads. In the hotel, a three-star hotel, you have to pay first before they give the room. When I wanted to pay in dollars they refused to accept them, and asked me to go and change them in a bank. They did not even bother to send someone to change, so I had to do it myself. I would not have stayed, but the hotels in town were full, this one was the fourth one we tried.

We went sight seeing, and naturally we visited the famous Shimbashi towers. We bought some souvenirs, including a miniature of the Shimbashi towers. I have it 'til this day. Then we went to the so-called electronic center. We bought some presents for our family. Personally I did not like Japan as it was now. I only hoped that China was as it was when I left her.

We stayed only two days in Tokyo, our next stop was Seoul, Korea. There the people seemed more hospitable, but the food was inedible, the worst Asian food I ever came across, in my opinion of course. My habit was and is that when I come to a new country, the first thing I do is to try the local food, and believe me I understand Asian food, so we had to go and look for Chinese restaurants or European food. There we stayed also for two days. Now I was eager to go to China as soon as possible.

I told my wife that we should bypass Taiwan, (Taiwan belongs to the nationalist China under the flag that I was born. During the Chinese civil war with the communists the nationalist government retreated to this island which was called before Formosa by a Portuguese discoverer some time in the Middle Ages.) and go straight to Hong Kong, but the plane we were on had to stop at Taipei, the capital of Taiwan.

When we arrived we had to go to the restaurant and wait for new passengers. On our way there, I looked up and saw the national flag of Taiwan, I was completely stunned. The flag on the mast was the flag under which I was born, and grew up with, it never occurred to me that I shall ever see this flag again. It is impossible to describe my feelings, now I know what is to be born and grow up in a country, even though you may be a Gypsy.

On the way to Hong Kong it was very bumpy, but thank God it was a short trip. When we were beginning to land, the plane gave a very sharp turn to the left, then it somehow came out of it. The landing in itself was the worse landing I ever experienced in my life. Not only me but the whole plane was on the verge of panic. When the plane finally stopped, the captain spoke over the mike, and said that it was not his fault, that a typhoon was on its way to Hong Kong, and the winds were almost eighty kilometers an hour, and he apologized for the inconvenience. When we left the plane to go to the waiting bus, the wind was truly very strong, I heard someone saying that we were lucky that we landed in time, because the wind seemed to get harder every minute that passed. When we arrived at the hotel, I asked, for curiosity, if they have any alarms on the airports when there is about to be a typhoon. "Yes," said the manager of the hotel, "In all they have eight flags to be unfurled, that is the highest point, now," he said, "they have unfurled only three, the television has just announced." Then he added, "I hope they don't raise any more flags, otherwise we will have a hard time even in the city, but sometimes it changes its course the very last minute, and everything gets well again." And it was exactly what happened, after a few hours the wind subsided, the typhoon took another course, and Hong Kong was saved from a natural disaster.

The very next morning we took a ferry boat from Hong Kong, from Kowloon (Kowloon is on the mainland of China, while Hong Kong is an island), and from there, a fast boat that takes an hour to get to Macao, a Portuguese colony. That's where my relatives lived, some of them since 1950, the last ones in China. What I noticed in Hong Kong, that the Chinese were far more better dressed than the tourists. The Chinese majority were dressed in suits and ties while the foreign tourists wore mostly jeans and ordinary T-shirts, and so did their women. It was just the opposite since the last time I was there. I could feel the climate has changed and not for the better.

We had their address, we took a taxi and arrived at their apartment with no trouble. They were of course waiting for us for quite a while, they thought that we would come directly to Hong Kong. I must explain to the reader that Macao has no airport, they were beginning to build one. When they saw us we could see the relief on their faces. We lost four days seeing Tokyo and Seoul.

The first thing they did was to take us to a typical Peking restaurant. The Chinese food from China has an absolutely different taste, because the vegetables are from the Chinese soil, even the meat has a different taste. What I liked more was the Peking duck, it has been a long time since I tasted this particular dish. To me there is only one place away from China that the Chinese food is very similar, it is in San Francisco, but of course the variety of dishes is only in China.

Macao is very small, to call it a city, it has no more than a dozen of streets. The town lives mostly of gambling and night life, and of course prostitution, there is also a lot of smuggling going on. I know this because one of my relatives is an inspector of the local police. In time he told me all about it. Besides all this, there was white slavery going on. From throughout the world white women are imported to Macao and Hong Kong. There were especially Russian women, coming down from Vladivostok, Russia, to work in bordellos and nightclubs; they made a lot of money. I myself talked to some of them. During the day there was a restaurant where these girls used to gather to have lunch, so my relative and I went there one day, just for curiosity and talk a little in Russian to them, to ask them how was life in Russia, after the breakdown of communism. One said, "If it would have been good, what do you think we are doing here? Most of us are here to make quick money, and go home to our parents as soon as possible. The work we do is not easy. When the night falls we have to go to work, they don't ask us if we are sick or in a bad mood, all they want us is to work, and we get only thirty percent after the whole night's work." She quickly added, "Please don't tell anybody what I have just told you, or else we might get in trouble, I trust you because you are a Russian." Then I corrected her. I said, "You will be surprised what I will tell you, for your information I am a Gypsy." She looked surprised and said, "You Gypsies are everywhere, and now I know that our secrets are safe with you. As far as I know, you Gypsies never sell out each other." "We started to laugh. I said, "Thank you for the compliment." Then she changed the subject and began to ask me what I and my friend was doing here. Not to prolong the story, I said that we are refugees from China, and that my parents were from Russia, that seemed to satisfy her curiosity. In all they were very good looking girls, mostly in their twenties. I felt a certain pity for them. I knew that they were exploited, but I did not want to go back to this subject, because I could not do nothing to help them. I only hoped that they do their jobs well, so that they may not be punished. If they don't, I have heard from many sources, that in some cases, if they don't do what they are told to do, they are severely beaten, and even murdered. I could only say, "Take care of yourselves." I knew that they knew that they were involved with a powerful crime organization, and were scared stiff, so we bid them goodbye, and promised to come again some day and have lunch with them. Of course I did not intend to keep my promise, and with that I satisfied my curiosity.

I told my relatives that I bought some extra tickets to nearby cities, but they wanted us to stay longer with them. I said, "We will stay until you will get tired of us," jokingly. Oh yes, we had a good time, especially in Hong Kong. We went to nightclubs, we went to buy things, but what I enjoyed more was of course the food. The smell of the food in the restaurants reminded me so much of my youth, but some things changed. The same thing happened here as in Japan, prosperity has gave them a status higher than they are supposed to be. The majority is not simple any more, they consider themselves superior to any other nation, and that spoils the China I used to know, that is my opinion of course. I wanted to go to Shanghai, but after what I saw in Hong Kong, I changed my mind. I did not want to spoil my good memories of Shanghai.

My relatives promised that they will come to visit us as soon as they can. They wanted to apply for a permanent visa to Brazil, because time was becoming short, before the communists will arrive soon. We also promised that we will try to help them in Brazil, via the foreign office, in case they don't get the visa. When time came for us to leave, we were all naturally sad, but what to do, life is such. I told them that today it is a small world, that we will see each other soon, and I thanked them very much for their generosity.

And so we left for Singapore, to my surprise I could not believe that this was Singapore, it was a completely different city. There was nothing there that I could recognize, the city was and is one of the most beautiful cities in Asia. No wonder they call the city the pearl of the East. The city is full of parks, and big avenues snake through them. There are very few shops on the sidewalks because the city is full of modern shopping centers. There was a street once known as Buggy Street, it was famous because hundreds of small restaurants were gathered together on the sidewalks of the street, and served the best Chinese food. It was the favorite meeting place of the tourists. I visited it myself the last time I was there, so I asked the taxi to take me there. To my surprise he said, "All right." I was sure it did not exist any more, but when we arrived, there was only five to six restaurants left. Nevertheless we went to one of them and had our dinner. Then I went and asked the owner, "Where are the rest of the restaurants?" He said that the government is building a new place for them and that the street will be demolished very soon. We stayed there for almost a week and loved every minute of it.

Our next stop was Thailand, Bangkok. This city I did not like, it was very dirty, and the people were practically rude, we did not understand a word of their language. The only thing I liked was the sightseeing. There were a lot of Buddhist temples to see, and their local dancers were very colorful and exotic. I knew they had precious stones, like blue sapphire, or even good rubies, but when I went to ask about the price, they were all above the world market prices. The ones I am writing about, of course, are the best that money could buy, so I ended up not buying even a single stone.

We took a direct plane to Seoul, Korea. From there we changed planes right at the airport. Of course, we waited for almost five hours, than across the whole Pacific Ocean, to Los Angeles, USA. There we had to stay overnight in a hotel, which the company of the airport took care of. The next day early in the morning we were off for home.

This time my family met us at airport, and I was very happy to see them. The trip lasted almost a month. In the meantime I gained almost five kilos, I was almost ninety kilos. Only in my youth I was that much, for the first in my life I felt tired, when I walked a few hundred miters. I did not know it then, but something bad was about to happen. Luckily me and my wife and my whole family have an health care plan, which I was paying religiously for almost ten years, a health security plan, the best doctors are working for this organization. One evening I begun to have pains in my stomach. I thought it was indigestion, but it persisted. I drank all kinds of antacid medicines, but it did not get better, so my wife and my sons, I don't remember which ones, they saw that I was suffering because the pain was getting unbearable. They took me to a doctor near my house. When he took my pressure, and then the electrocardiogram of the heart, he immediately told my wife to take me as soon as possible to the hospital. That night I suffered as I did never before in my life. I don't remember much of the night, but what I remember was the next morning they took me up to the room. I was so doped up that I could hardly open my eyes. Later that afternoon that doctor came. He said that I did not have an heart attack, but I had what they call angina, which means that some veins in my heart were blocked, and that they must make another exam, to see how much damage this has done to my heart. The exam is terrible, they dope you up again, then they open the main vein in your arm, and push in a wire with a miniature TV camera, attach to it up 'til the heart, and then they see my heart on television, and also take pictures. It was not painful, the dope must have neutralized it. I had to wait for the exam to know if I have to be operated, in the meantime I was heavily medicated. I stayed about ten days in the hospital. I came home, but I was still weak. After a few days the doctor told me to come and see him, so that he may give me the decision to operate or not. On my way to him I was very nervous, but I had a pill that calmed me down, so when I arrived I was as calm as a kitten. I will never forget the conversation we had. He simply said, "Your case is not too dangerous. You have two little veins that are blocked, but if you won't make a bypass, later on you may have serious trouble, so I advise you to make this operation. You need only two bypasses. The doctor who will operate is one of the best in the country. His name is doctor Adib Jateni. But before you make the operation, I want you to have another opinion." He gave me the address of the other doctor, and even marked a consultation for me, and then to phone to tell him what have we decided. I have heard of doctor Adib Jateni before, he was the best that money could buy. Thanks God I was secured, I did not have to pay a red cent for the operation. The other doctor saw the film which I have borrowed from the hospital, he also confirmed what the other doctor said, he openly said that I was too young to die. I asked him straight, what were my chances to live. He said, to my surprise 98 percent, he also said the doctor Adib Jateni won't let me down. So I have been operated. It is a complete success, my doctor, Adib Jateni, lived to become twice the Minister of the Health Department of Brazil and is still is considered the best authority on the health system of the country. But nevertheless I have to take drugs for the rest of my life, to keep me going. It's been seven years now and I still have to see a doctor every three months to check my blood pressure, etc., etc.

Oh yes, I am still active, and even have some drinks every now and then, but one thing is for sure, I am far from normal. I have to exercise or just walk as much as I can, but not to get too tired. Every year that passes I walk less and less, but God is good, he is always there when I need Him. I have just had my sixty-fifth birthday, on the eighth of March, the International Women's Day. I sometimes wonder why I have been born on this specific day. The answer is that women are the most wonderful creatures that God has ever created on the face of this earth. My hobby was, and still is, believe it or not, is to appreciate the beauty of a woman.

Now I wish to write about my children. My son Latsi, the eldest, lives in Santa Barbara, a hundred and fifty kilometers west of São Paulo, and is happily married to his wife Regina, a Brazilian, but from Spanish descent. They are married for over twenty years. He has three daughters, which I have named them earlier in this book, they all go to school, and the eldest will graduate shortly. He works very hard to support his family and so does his wife. I hardly ever see him, only on special occasions, like my birthday, and of course Christmas. He and my youngest daughter usually speak to me in Gypsy, the rest prefer to speak in Brazilian, but I have learned to respect their preference. Latsi is a very intelligent man. He is the one who really fought in life to get what he has today. Although his is well off he never shows off. He is very simple, and is the best in telling jokes, and also has a memory of an elephant. There is no Brazilian popular songs that he says that he does not know the lyrics. That makes him indispensable on our parties.

After my son comes my daughter Zina, she is a very beautiful and also a determined women. When she wants something she does anything in her power to get it. Her husband comes from a good family. His father, Durval Kohn, is one of the few Brazilians that I consider my good friend. Zina is one of those women who is very hard to analyze, but, however, up 'til now I did not have any problems with her, as a matter of fact she seems to be the one who worries more about our family. She is always there when any of the family needs her, in all our domestic problems. She has a beautiful daughter which is very intelligent. Of course I don't want to undermine my other grandchildren. I love them all, I consider them the continuation of my life.

Then comes Tsino, he is the most sensitive person in my family. His wife Rosy also comes from European descent. She also helps her husband as she can in his work. They seem to be doing well. They have two children, a son and a daughter, his son is the only male grand son that I have. Tsino is a good guitar player, but he plays it as a hobby. He is the only one that I see almost daily, because as representative of a medical firm he uses my house as his office, and when he needs his computer, which is almost daily, he comes to his office. Tsino is a person that is very hard not to get on with, he makes friends very easily. He hardly ever argues with anyone, I never saw him to lose his temper, and is loved by all of us due to his character. My father used to be like that. I only wish to God that his son will be like him.

Now comes my daughter Olga, the youngest of my children. She is the only one that traveled with me and my wife for some time. Recently Olga has given us a lot of worry. She found out that she had a few very small tumors on her neck. We all told her to go and check. My wife went with her, she made some exams, and we waited for the result. When it came, it came like a bombshell, the tumors were malignant, and it was situated right on her thyroid gland, it was to be removed immediately. The doctor said that this type of cancer is very easily cured when it's still in an early condition, that he has done many operations in similar conditions, and was a complete success. The father of my son-in-law, Tais, had exactly the same case ten to fifteen years ago, and is still doing fine. That doctor also said, that if one day he should have cancer, he would want it to be the type that Olga had. And so she operated. It was a complete success. All she had to do was take some radioactive medicine, and isolated for a few days, and that was it, as far as the cancer was concerned. But for the thyroid gland she will have to take a pill a day for the rest of her life. It is almost a year since she operated, thanks God she is fine, but every year she must make a check up, just to make sure that nothing is wrong with her. Olga gave us a big scare, she was never seriously sick through out her young life, but recently she is even allergic to a ant's bite. Due to all this confusion her character has changed, and not for the better, but thank God, little by little, she seems to get over it. I am very proud of her, she and her husband Cilmar Fortes, are both lawyers and doing fine.

I can thank my lucky star that God has given me and my wife such good children, none of them smoke or drink. My sons drink, but only socially. All of them are independent, and up 'til now we did not have major troubles.

Just to give my reader an example, my sister's son has given me more trouble than my sons. He married three women, two Gypsies and one from Chile. With the Gypsy women he has a daughter. With the Chilean he has three children, one son and two daughters. With the other Gypsy woman he did not have any children, but he could not manage to stay with any of them. Now he is all alone for almost seven years. Every now and then he comes to me when he is low on cash, so I have to bail him out, but this is just one of his misdeeds. Here among our Gypsies I have a certain respect, and being a godfather, to a Gypsy is a very serious thing, they consider you as a relative, but my nephew many times went to their homes, and got drunk and talked nonsense. Thanks to me he was not beaten, all this and even much more, which I don't even want to mention, has broken my relationship with him, but never the less I know that he will appear again in my house, and I will have to help him again and again as I did throughout these years.

As far as I am concerned, again I must say that someone up there likes me a lot, for I am fortunate to have a wife like Maita, the ever-faithful wife, for giving me such a wonderful family. I must confess that in my youth I was no saint, I gave my wife a lot of trouble throughout our marriage, and some how we went through it for forty-two years, and thanks God we are still going strong.

Times have changed, tradition is almost gone. I personally would not like to be young at this times, everybody talks about love or passion, but as I see it, there is nothing but a materialistic world. To be romantic today is to be a fool, to pull a chair for a lady is to be laughed at, to take to dinner a lady and pay the check, she most probably will be offended, instead she would ask you to pay half of the check. In the old days things were different. When I ask someone or some people to dinner or a night-club, I pay the check without even letting them know, that's how I was taught by my father.

Yes, even Gypsies change. Today mostly everyone wants to outwit the other, nothing is taboo. Honestly, I don't know how far this type of living can go. Even we Gypsies have our differences, one tribe hates another just because a hundred of years ago in Russia or somewhere else in this world they had a fight on a wedding or some other festival occasion, and one of the parties got killed in the fight. This will never be forgotten, their children's children are told about their misfortune, and are told to fight this tribe whenever they happen to see them. This is what I call an ethnic war in miniature.

Today I am not surprised at the Jewish-Arabic conflict, their hatred is too deeply rooted, for thousands of years they are enemies. I think it is a waste of time and energy. To try and bring them to live side by side, my opinion is to divide them completely, and always have a foreign force on the border of their respective countries, to keep the peace. Not only these countries but wherever are the ethnic wars, like Bosnia, Croatia, etc., etc., should do the same. Today as I see it, Christians and Muslims can live in other countries together which is not their own, like Brazil for instance, here they behave, because the government is not theirs, and manage to live side by side. Sometimes I wonder why the Jewish people were and are condemned by so many countries for thousand of years, and yet they are called as the chosen people of God. What they went through these thousands of years only God knows, and God is merciful! I don't think they deserved these sufferings, not only them but any other people in this world, which automatically brings me back to my people, the Gypsies, we also suffered and suffer some sort of discrimination, but nothing compared to the Jewish people. Only in wartime Germany our Gypsies were killed, because they were just Gypsies. I have never heard of mass killings of my people in any other countries.

There is a legend about my people which I have heard in India and will relate it to my reader. Once upon a time there was a state in India whose people were happy, prosperous, and their standard of living was higher than the other states surrounding them. Their main activities were utensils made out of copper, and, of course, music, besides many others things. We were a very small state. We did not even have an army to protect us because we had no known enemies. We were famous even outside of our country. Merchants used to come from far off to buy our goods, and mostly to enjoy our music, and also to tell them their fortune. We were considered to be good at that. As you can see, we had a lot of good things to offer to our tourists, and in no time we were better off than the others. That is where envy and greed came in. Since we had no warriors we were a easy target. And than one day we were attacked and nearly completely destroyed. Those who escaped are now known as Gypsies. In time we were all scattered throughout the world.

The trouble with my people was and is that we had no writings to tell the story because we were all uneducated. Up 'til today we have no writings of our own. It does not exist, as far as I know. That is why during the second World War the numbers of the Jewish victims who were killed are known, but the Gypsy casualties are unknown, because we were not classified anywhere. The number officially given is not correct. They estimate that about two hundred thousand were killed, but I see a bigger number.

'Til today the German government is paying some money monthly to those families who lost their loved ones in the war; those are mostly German Gypsies. I have seen them personally, they complain that out of ten families only three to four are recognized as victims of the war, the rest have no way to prove it, due to their ignorance. One of the leaders of the Gypsy community in Germany even went to complain to the holy Pope Paul the Second, but to no avail, even though he promised that he will try and do something about it.

I have noted one thing about our Gypsies, there is almost no connections between the tribes today. Very rarely they unite, only when there is some serious questions to be decided. Otherwise every tribe keeps its distance from the other. At least that's how it is in Brazil.

As far as my sons and daughters are concerned, they try to avoid the local Gypsies as much as possible. I don't blame them, because I am to blame in a way. Since they were children I told them that our tribe was completely different from those of Kelderasa or Machvaya. Our way of living is very similar to those of Gaje, which means a stranger. Sometimes I regret what I said to them, but it is too late to change them now.

What I want to transmit to the reader is that now that I am of advanced age, I personally miss the old Gypsy way of life. In China we were almost united, and I mean all the tribes that lived there. We never passed a Christmas or any other holiday without each other. But those times are gone forever, and with it the Gypsy way of life. Today particularly the youngsters, even of the most radical Gypsies, the tradition, the rules, the culture, is dying out. At least this is what is happening in Brazil, if not throughout the world. But thank God I have managed to see almost all the tribes in this world.

Sometimes I wonder why the United Nations does not try to find out whether we Gypsies want to unite and form a nation. After all we are estimated as many as twenty million people today. There are countries who are recognized by the United Nations, some of them have less than a million population, like Luxembourg etc., etc. I think this act would be a miracle for the Gypsies, a dream that might come true. As for the leadership, this will be a problem, we have very little amount of highly educated people to form a government. Although I have heard that in Russia we had Gypsy officers in the Red Army during the war in high positions, and also doctors, lawyers, etc., etc. Such people could form a government. But then, there is too much hatred and ethnic wars are going on among some nations in this world today, there is no time for the United Nations to even think about forming a new nation. Maybe someday this dream of mine, and millions of others Gypsies will come true.

Finally, I am proud to announce to my reader that one of our Gypsies is one step from being canonized by the Pope Paul the Second. There was a very big gathering on the Saint Peter's Square especially for this occasion. The Gypsy is called El Pele, which means a strong man. His real name was Ceferino Jiminez Malla, a Spanish Gypsy. He was a horse trader and very honest and religious, some were around Barbastro, Spain. He became very popular with the Gypsies in the region, and also with the Gaje, which means strangers, for being deeply religious. He was arrested in July 1936 by an anti-clerical militia after he publicly, defended a priest. When asked whether he had any weapons, he extracted a rosary from his pocket. He was killed at the age of seventy-five with a number of other priests by a firing squad, by forces opposed to General Francisco Franco. El Pele died for the faith that he lived out. The Pope said his life showed how our God Jesus Christ is present in various people and races, and that all people are called holiness. Now this is something good for our people, this beatification was realized on the fourth of May 1997. I watched it on the TV, on the CNN channel and later on the internet. Four hundred million people watch this network, at least what the network says. At last we have conquered a space among the nations in this world. To me it is a great event, who knows, in time the dream that I wrote about will come true.

The announcer also said that during the war half a million Gypsies have lost their lives, this proves what I have wrote, that nobody really knows the exact number of the executions that took place of the Holocaust.

As for the religious part of my people, they are very serous about it, no matter if he or she is Catholic or Muslim, Orthodox, etc., etc., but they are not fanatic about it. Of course there are always a few exceptions, they are in a minority.

Now I would like to write about the Gypsies, not only of Brazil but around the world. Basically our customs are very similar with a few exceptions. Now in this modern world the differences are great. The big change started to manifest itself after the second World War. I have already mentioned to the reader earlier in my book about my people, what type of work these people do. For instance, the family which I always am in contact is the family of my godson. His father, Roberto Ivanoff, he works with all kind of industrial tools, which he repairs them. Mostly all the Gypsies of Russian descent do this type of work, while their women tell fortune when ever possible. Let's say these are the middle-class society. But the rich are car dealers, house builders, even some lawyers, and also some doctors. But these people are mostly from the Machvaya tribe, they are from Yugoslavian descent.

Whenever I am invited to a wedding or some feast by the Gypsies of Brazil, I am always treated differently, I think because I represent the one and only Lovara tribe in this country, and I am proud about it. For thirty-seven years I have never had a quarrel with any of these tribes. On the contrary, we live in peace and harmony side by side. But as far as they are concerned there is always some misunderstandings going on between them, especially whenever some family wants a daughter-in-law and the father of the girl does not want his daughter in that particular family. Or when the youngsters get together and get in a fight, etc., etc. After this type of acts, there is always a gathering and the persons involved are to be judged by the elders. I was sometimes called to this type of meeting but I refused to go under any circumstances. Once I went just to tell them that our Lovara's law is different from theirs, so I don't find myself competent to judge anybody unless he or she is from my tribe. Since then they have never bothered me again.

Now I am almost retired, once in a blue moon my ex-customers come to me to make business. At my age to travel is not an easy task. Maybe if I have not been operated on, things would have been different. But I am happy because my children are in good health, particularly my youngest daughter Olga, recently she went through a full health check up, and was pronounced hundred percent healthy. My only wish now is to visit Moscow Russia, and see my other part of relatives. I am working on it, that is to persuade my wife on the trip, she is a hard nut to crack, but I think I will succeed. With God's help anything is possible.

I have written in this book the main events of my life. I think that God is good to me and my family, I only regret that I could not do more for my sisters, or even my nephews, and relatives, especially those who are in need. Today, as the saying goes, that God helps those who helps themselves.

I would not do justice to my reader or to me if I will not relate the story of my parents or the people who had the most influence on my life. Of course, what I am about to write was related to me by my father. Actually, our tribe is originally from Hungary. For some reason or another they immigrated to Iran. My grandfather was born in Iran. By they, I mean my grandfather's clan. He was called O Baro Gurano which means the big Gurano, this was his name. He was a born leader, strong, rich, and handsome, everything a man wanted in life. He had almost twenty to thirty families under his command. At those times he was considered their absolute leader. They traveled from town to town, country to country, they lived in tents. Their women told fortunes while the men dealt with horses, this was their main activities. His wife was Roza, my grandmother. She bore him two sons and three daughters, my father was the third. He was born also in Iran, in Tabriz to be exact, the capital of Azerbaidjan, some time in 1894.

Now my father jumps fourteen years ahead, he remembers very well, because it was his wedding day. It seems that my grandfather met some other clan, and saw a beautiful young Gypsy girl, and decided to marry my father to her. The girl was about eighteen years old and my father was only fourteen. While the wedding was going on, my father was hunting birds in the forest with a sling shot. And to think, that he stayed two to three years with her. This event was already in Russia, the town, he said, was Cheliabinsk, Siberia.

On my mother's side, my grandfather's name was Latsi. He was not a big man but very intelligent. He also had his clan. I named my first son after him. Of course, we were all Lovara tribe and related to each other. He was the only one who had education to some degree.

When he was invited to some feast or a wedding and the big Gurano was also present, he came always armed with a gun, because Gurano was always a potential danger when he drank. It was said that on one occasion, he alone destroyed a whole camp of Gypsies, he was drunk of course. He beat up about a half a dozen. The rest went to hide in the forest, so he destroyed their camp, this is one reason he was known and feared throughout Russia by the Gypsies.

I personally remember him. At that time he was about eighty-five years old. He looked like a giant to me, he was about two meters tall and still very strong. I did not see my other grandfather.

My mother, Katusha was her name, was about to marry my father, so my grandfather and his two sons went to another city, where my mother lived, to make the arrangements for the wedding, but when they arrived, there was another clan of Gypsies trying to ask the hand of my mother. When this clan saw my grandfather and his sons, immediately in the camp there was confusion. The clan knew that my mother was already promised to my father, but still they insisted to ask the hand of my mother. Without thinking twice, my grandfather, my father, and his brother found some heavy clubs, and came out to face about twenty-odd, male Gypsies who in turn, were waiting for them to fight it out. The rest is history, even a song was composed by a Gypsy about the event, they completely destroyed the clan who faced them. The rest ran into the forest. Some of them were seriously hurt, and their wives went to complain to the police, but my father picked up all their hats and showed them to the police. The officer was stunned, so many against three, so the officer chased their wives out of the police station. Then my grandfather took my mother by the hand and took her away to be married to my father.

Sergei and Katarina Vishnevsky, Siberia, 1920s. (Courtesy of the author.)

My parents lived in Cheliabinsk. My mother bore my father two sons and four daughters. Only me and my sister Zina were born in China. The rest were born in Russia as Iranian citizens. My father did not want them to be Russian citizens because of the civil war.

During the civil war there was widespread hunger. Throughout Russia, my father said, you could see dead people on the streets, swollen up by decay, and there was nobody to bury them. At that time some areas in Siberia were occupied by White Russian troops, and were not very far from each other. That's were my father stepped in. He used to trade horses for food. He traveled at night to the White Russian area with some horses, and made the transaction for food. That's how we survived, but then he got caught, and was about to be shot. If not for the Gypsy communist officer he would have been dead, and this book would have not been written, for the simple reason that I had not been born yet.

So we had to run, the nearest border was China, that's how we got there, and that's were I was born. But not only we were on the run, thousands of Russians, and a few thousand Gypsies were in the same spot as us, for one reason or another, but mostly I think was from the lack of food in Russia. Of course there were many officers of ex-Imperial Russian army, including generals, high officials, etc., etc.

But what troubled my father most was that my grandfather could not adapt himself to the Chinese way of life. But there was no return, and he knew it. Thanks to the Russian immigrants we always had work in the nightclubs. I even remember their names. One was by the name of Kavkaz, the other was Renaissance. Both were very luxurious nightclubs and were on the main street of the French Concession. Only the rich had access to these clubs. This was in Shanghai during the second World War.

Yes we also had our collaborators working for the Japanese, mostly White Russians, who made a fortune during the war. God knows what happened to them after the war, they just disappeared, the ones who worked for the local police. I have heard that they were punished.

In Russia we left behind two houses that my grant father owned. They are still there, I was told by my relatives in Stockholm.

In Shanghai, the new generation of my family were almost all born at the same hospital, I was born there, it was named the Saint Mary's. Believe it or not, I remember when my wife Maita was brought home from the hospital. I was eight years old. My brother, his name was Surro, was very sick. He had a sickness called arthritis, but at that time the doctors did not even have the name of this sickness. He could not walk. We tried every thing in our power to cure him, but to no avail. My mother and father, even took him to the Philippines for him to bathe in the warm volcanic sulfur waters. It worked for a while. He even walked, but when they came back in Shanghai, it started all over again. There was a doctor, very well known, and said to be the best for such cases, he said that he should be operated on both legs, one at a time. The first operation went well, but the second was fatal. The chloroform which was used on him to sleep was so strong that it killed him. He was only twenty years old. The impact of this tragedy was so hard that my father said that he will kill the doctor. When the doctor saw a crowd of Gypsies gathering outside of the hospital, he fled from the back door, not only from the hospital but from Shanghai. He must have been warned that the Gypsies were coming to get him. He was gone, never to be seen again. The mourning of his death was such that it even appeared in the Russian news paper—it was called the *Zaria*—because there were almost a hundred people gathered at my house. They were from all the tribes of Gypsies. My mother did not eat or drink for several days. Only when they brought me to her and told her that she still has something to live for, then and only then, she had a sip of orange juice. We Gypsies mourn our dead, particularly those who die young, very severely, the crying goes on day and night. There must be someone, not a relative, to take care of the parents of the victim, because nobody knows what he or she might do to themselves physically, like slap their faces, or beat their heads on a wall, and sometimes try to throw themselves under a car. Today it's different, but still when someone is seriously sick, even here in São Paulo they gather at the hospital, not by the hundreds, but enough to be thrown out of the hospital for disturbing the peace.

Today only my sister Zina and me are the oldest of my tribe in Brazil, and I feel very sad about it. I miss my generation, I sometimes dream about my old friends who are now gone forever, although we had some troubles between us, but nothing serious that we could not work out.

If my reader would ask me, where of all these countries that I passed, I liked it best, I will certainly say Brazil first, then comes China, and the good old USA. Brazil is the country that I spent the most of my lifetime, and never regretted it. I think that I am very lucky to live in a country, where the future is just starting. Here, I think, we are all far away from the troubles of the world.

I hope it stays that way in the future. Don't get me wrong, I did not say that I want this country to be isolated from the other countries. What I want it to be is truly democratically free to its people and neutral as far as other countries are concerned.

Victor and Maita Vishnevsky at the book-signing for the Portuguese version, 1999. (Courtesy of the author.)

The author and family, 2006. (Courtesy of the author.)

Salo Press publishes autobiographical works by Gypsies, presented in the author's own words.

SALO
PRESS

5607 Greenleaf Road
Cheverly MD 20785
USA

SAN 851-5913